An Introduction To Smallholdings

Getting Started On Your Smallholding

Jason Johns

Visit me at www.GardeningWithJason.com for gardening tips and advice or follow me at www.YouTube.com/OwningAnAllotment for my video diary and tips. Join me on Facebook at www.Facebook.com/OwningAnAllotment.

Follow me on Instagram and Twitter as @allotmentowner for regular updates, tips and to ask your gardening questions.

If you have enjoyed this book, please leave a review. I read each review personally and the feedback helps me to continually improve my books.

© 2021 Jason Johns

All rights reserved.

TABLE OF CONTENTS

Why Become a Smallholder? 1

Choosing A Smallholding Site 8

What To Grow On Your Smallholding 14

Crop Rotation For Smallholders...29

Keeping Livestock..33

Reducing Your Environmental Impact...................................44

Structures and Equipment..53

Earning An Income From Your Smallholding 61

Endnote 68

About Jason 71

Other Books By Jason 73

Want More Inspiring Gardening Ideas? 79

Free Book!..80

Why Become a Smallholder?

Many people dream of escaping the rat race and living in the countryside, self-sufficient on their own smallholding. According to some research, this is a dream around half the population of the UK have, though with the Covid-19 crisis in 2020, this figure has probably increased significantly.

People want to become a smallholder for a variety of reason, including living a more sustainable and healthy life, to retire to and as a way to live in the countryside and have an income. Becoming a smallholder is considered to be a better way of life by many people and a chance to get back to nature.

When it comes to turning this dream into a reality, the cost of setting up a smallholding is prohibitive for many people. The reality is that owning a smallholding isn't like the 70's TV show "The Good Life", with all fun and laughs. While it can be a lot of fun, it can be a lot of work, requiring you to learn new skills and balance your smallholding life with your family life. Becoming a smallholder is a 365 day a year job, being outside in every weather and often at all times of day, particularly if you own livestock.

While the dream of becoming a smallholder is fantastic, only around a quarter of smallholders report their land generates an income, so it is important that before becoming a smallholder you plan how you are going to become self-sufficient.

A smallholding is your own piece of heaven in the countryside. It is larger than a garden but smaller than a farm, usually several acres and sometimes as much as 40 or 50 acres. Depending on your space, you may just grow vegetables or could keep livestock.

It is a residential site, with a home, and an area of land for growing vegetables and keeping livestock. With a smallholding, you are producing food for yourself and your family, and often producing more than you need to sell. Often smallholdings will have a woodland area which is managed by the smallholder to provide fuel for fires or to sell. A smallholding can be a single family, but it is not unheard of for a group of people to pool their resources to create a smallholding and share the work and rewards.

Smallholdings can be very productive, often more so than farms because an area of land is used for a variety of different purposes. For example, an orchard could contain bees and chickens with some herbs under the trees too. Farms tend to focus on monoculture, meaning the same orchard on a farm would just be for growing fruit.

A smallholder typically tries their best to live in harmony with nature and reduce their environmental impact. Smallholding practices mean the soil is in good condition and they work with companion planting and other natural methods to reduce the need for chemicals. Due to the nature of a smallholding, biodiversity is greater because there is a wider variety of plants in a small area.

Smallholdings are often run by a single family, but during busy times, they will often hire local people to help with the work. Many local people prefer to buy local too, which benefits the smallholder.

It isn't necessarily easy to make a living from a smallholding, but it isn't any different from earning an income from a farm. The jobs on a smallholding are varied and are physically and mentally demanding. Owning a smallholding isn't a job, but a way of life. It is hard work, but it is very rewarding to realise that you are self-sufficient!

Tips for Smallholding Success

It is possible to succeed as a smallholder and if you make a plan and do your research, you are much more likely to succeed. These tips will help you make your smallholding successful:

- Keep Records – it is important as a business, which your smallholding is, to keep records. Track what you grow, where you grow it and the harvest quantities. Keep track of the weather and animal health too. On top of this, you have to keep track of your income and outgoings.

- Be Positive – you are going to get good and bad years. One year, you may struggle to get your vegetables to grow but the next year you could have a bumper harvest. Some of your livestock could die, storms can cause damage or you could suffer from flooding. The important thing is to stay positive and know that it is all part of the natural cycle of life and you will have some setbacks. A positive attitude helps significantly in tackling these issues and overcoming them.
- Educate Yourself – if you haven't got any experience running a smallholding, then it can be a daunting task. It is very different from owning a house and having a back garden. Take time to educate yourself both before you take on your smallholding and after you have taken it on. Keep abreast of new developments and methods, find out about different types of plants and breeds of animal. Listen to people with experience and learn everything you can as it will make owning a smallholding much easier.
- Invest in a Polytunnel – one of these or a greenhouse are essential for a smallholder as they allow you to grow crops that you would not otherwise be able to grow. They extend your growing season and provides delicate crops such as tomatoes and peppers some protection from the elements. While these can be a costly investment, they can often be found cheap in the second hand market. Just make sure they are securely fixed to prevent damage from the elements.
- Windbreaks – depending on where your smallholding is located, a windbreak could help give your crops and buildings some protection from the elements. Plant trees (native are best) along field edges to act as a windbreak and to provide homes for wildlife.
- Get Involved – there is a large smallholder community these days and it is worth getting involved with it both online and in your local area. Talking to people who have been through the journey you are planning to undertake can help you avoid some pitfalls and learn more about smallholding. It is a close community and can be helpful when you encounter problems or need help.
- Make Your Home Nice – a part of a smallholding that is not often considered is the part you live in … your home. It is important that this is made into a nice environment that you can enjoy returning to after working outside. It is important to have this refuge for you and your family.
- Stay Focused – don't try to take on too much at once. Smallholding

is a marathon, not a race. Avoid focusing on too many projects at one time and just focus on one or two main projects. For example, in the first year, you might set up your vegetable garden and fruit trees, then in the second livestock, then in the third convert outbuildings into holiday homes and in the fourth start keeping bees. Trying to take on too much means you can end up being overwhelmed and not getting anything completed.

- Don't Rush – be prepared to spend some time getting to know your soil, the local climate, the local area and the local farming/smallholding community. Knowing your soil and climate can help you know what to grow and talking to other smallholders can give you valuable insight into this.
- Invest in Fencing – good fencing can make a big difference to you. It can prevent the neighbour's animals getting onto your land and damaging your crops, keep out ramblers, keep your livestock in and ensure you know the limit of your land. Of course, fences can be productive too – fruit bushes, hazel trees and other fruit trees can all be planted along the fence.
- Good Clothing – with a smallholding you are going to be outside in all kinds of weather at all times of year. It is worth your while investing in good quality outdoor clothing, including winter wear and waterproofs. If you do not have this type of clothing, going out in bad weather, which you will have to do, becomes a major chore. It will keep you warm and dry and make working your land bearable in bad weather.
- Have Enough Land – it is easy to think you can 'make do' with an acre or half an acre of land, but as you get going, you will soon realise that you need more space. An orchard that produces enough fruit for you to use, store and sell takes up quite an area of land. Chickens and other livestock need space, and a good sized vegetable garden is required to produce enough to be self-sufficient. Always go for enough land that you can expand your operations – it doesn't matter if it lays fallow for a year or two, having the space to expand can be important as your smallholding grows.

Considerations Before Taking on a Smallholding

Taking on a smallholding is not a decision to take lightly and it is one that you must think through very carefully. There are a lot of things that you should consider, not least your family, your children, their schooling and opportunities for them. These are some things that you should consider before you take on a smallholding:

An Introduction to Smallholdings

- Try It First – taking on a smallholding is significant commitment, particularly if you have little experience growing vegetables or looking after livestock. Attend some smallholding or farming courses to get some experience of what a smallholding is like. This will give you an idea of whether it is for you or not. Try to speak to other smallholders and learn more about their experience. Follow blogs online and on social media to understand what smallholding involves.
- What Are Your Goals? – before starting a smallholding, you need to understand why you are doing it and what you are hoping to achieve from it. Are you looking to have a full-time job and transition to full-time smallholding gradually or jump in with both feet from day one? Are you looking to turn your smallholding into a full-time business? No matter how much you want to be away from civilisation, unless you have a plan, you can find yourself without an income. Starting a business, particularly one that involves growing vegetables or keeping animals, isn't something that happens overnight. You need to have a plan so you know you are secure. are working towards your goals and can make your smallholding work for you.
- Be Prepared For Work – a smallholding is not light work and, depending on what you have on yours, can be a lot of work and even involve anti-social hours such as lambing in the middle of the night. Don't underestimate how much time a smallholding is going to take. If you are planning on keeping a full-time job, be prepared for a lot of work in evenings and at weekends, meaning your TV schedule will take a hit! How much time you have will influence how much you can do on your smallholding. Make sure you are realistic in what you can achieve and know that your time in winter months will be limited due to weather and darkness.
- Start Small – unless you have some farming experience, going out and buying a 900-acre farm is going to cause you a serious headache as you do not know what you are doing. Certainly buy the amount

of land you want long term, but be realistic in what you can achieve. If you have never kept livestock before, buying a herd of cattle, a flock of sheep and chickens on day one will be overwhelming, so start with a few chickens and work your way up.

- Research Everything – and I mean, everything. You need to know what you want to grow because this will influence the type of land you need. If you want to keep livestock, then living on the side of a mountain isn't so much of a problem, but fruit and vegetables may not appreciate it as much. Pigs prefer woodland, while sheep prefer to be higher up. Think about what you are going to do with your smallholding and then find the ideal area. Researching will ensure you are armed with the right information to make the right decisions so that your smallholding is a success.

- Do The Paperwork – owning a smallholding involves quite a bit of paperwork. Not only do you need to complete your taxes, but you also need to fill in a lot of paperwork in order to keep livestock. You will need to register with DEFRA and also get a County Parish Holding Number. It will help you if you keep good records of what you grow, plus if you are selling anything, you will need to keep track of that too.

- Are You Up For The Work? – a smallholding is a lot of physical work, but is rewarding in many ways. However, are you up to it? If you suffer from long-term health issues, then you may not be able to do all the work yourself and may need to hire someone, which you will have to factor in to your running costs.

- Affordability – starting a smallholding isn't cheap. For starters, you have to buy the property itself, but then you have the cost of equipment and supplies. You may need machinery, seeds, plants, trees, tools, structures such as sheds, greenhouses or polytunnels, a 4x4 for getting around and more. Earning an income from a smallholding is not likely to happen from the start, unless you take over a going concern. It could be months or even a year or more before you see any income. If you are letting cottages, it can take a while for word to get out and you to get guests. Fruit trees can take several years before they produce a good yield while vegetables can take months before you can harvest them. Livestock can take a year or more before they are ready, though chickens can produce eggs in just a few months.

- Money To Keep You Going – while you are waiting for your smallholding to bring in some money, you need to have enough money to pay your bills and keep you going. Be aware that you will have to pay council tax plus you will get taxed on your earnings as a smallholder. You are also solely responsible for your pension contributions, any health care and all insurances. Unless you are generating your own electricity, you will have to pay for that, plus you will need to pay for gas or oil for heating. As it will take a while to build up your income from your land, you need to have enough money in the bank or a job, to ensure you can survive.

- Insurance – there are specific insurances you can take out to protect your crops and livestock as a smallholder. These could well be useful and are worth investigating. On top of this, you will need the usual insurances for your home and vehicles. Remember to include these costs in your planning.
- Family – you need to consider the rest of your family when buying your smallholding. If you have children, where are they going to go to school or college? Where are they going to play and what are they going to do? What about your spouse, if you have one? Are they working on the smallholding or working elsewhere? Owning a smallholding is a big decision that involves the whole family, so think about their needs as well.

Choosing A Smallholding Site

One of the most important decisions you will make is where your smallholding is located. This has an impact on you financially and on what you can grow as well as which animals you can keep. A smallholding in the Scottish Highlands has very different conditions to one located on the south coast of England. As this is your future, you need to make sure that you buy the right smallholding in the right place.

When you are choosing the site, there are a lot of things you need to think about, such as the following:

What Are Your Plans?
Are you planning to keep livestock, grow grapes for wine, grow vegetables, holiday lets, glamping or something different? This is going to have a major impact on your location and possibly your budget. If you are planning on relying on holiday lets, glamping or bed and breakfast for your income, then your smallholding needs to be in a location popular with tourists and travellers. If you are planning on selling produce, then you need to be located somewhere that has a market you can sell at and a good amount of people nearby that can buy from you.

Therefore, before you even start looking at locations, you should consider where your income is coming from. However, you may look at a location and think it is ideal and work out a way to make an income, but this is much rarer and has more risk associated with it.

Budget
How much you have to spend on your smallholding will impact where you can buy. Popular tourist locations are more expensive than more isolated communities, but the latter are harder for you to earn an income from. A smallholding near the coast in Cornwall will be far more expensive than one located in the Scottish Highlands.

Understand how much money you have to spend but make sure that you have enough money to survive on until your income streams are stable. Also know how far you can stretch your buying budget without impacting your budget for setting up the smallholding.

Climate
What is the local climate like? Is the smallholding in a location where it gets lots of sun, or does it lose the light early due to mountains? Is it in an area that is likely to be a frost pocket, or get flooded or get little rain? If you are growing vegetables, then the climate needs to be right for them. In a frost pocket, your growing season will be shortened. If you get flooded or get too little rain, that won't help vegetables and most vegetable plants need plenty of sun too. Livestock don't mind less sun, but they do object to regular flooding and some may dislike the cold. Look at weather data online for the past few years and ask around the local area if necessary.

Soil
It will help you to understand the soil on a potential site. Is it clay, sandy or a good quality loam? While you can amend a poor soil, it takes time that may delay you earning an income. Is the soil very stony? If it is, this can be cleared as it will make it harder to grow vegetables. Is the soil acidic or alkaline? A simple pH test will tell you this. If the soil is too acidic or too alkaline, then it can impact vegetable growing. Again, you can adjust the acidity of the soil, but it is extra work and cost.

Size
How much space do you need? Do you need 5 acres? 10? 20? More? If you are growing food to sell or keeping livestock, you will need more space than if you are just growing for yourself. Remember that it is better to get more land rather than get too little and not be able to expand. If you are not planning on using all of the land initially, you can look at renting it to local people to grow on or for equestrian use, which can provide another source of income.

Also, look at what the land comprises of. Is it level, sloping, pasture, wooded? If it is scrubland or wooded, then there will be a lot of work clearing it to make way for your vegetable garden or livestock. If it is steeply sloped, it will be difficult to work and will be expensive to level out or build terraces. Does it have a stream or river on the property? If it does, does this have a tendency to flood?

Access
What kind of access is there to the property? Is it a council road or a private road? If it is a private road then you and any other landowners with rights to it will be responsible for maintenance of the road, which is a cost you will have to factor into your budget. Can you get deliveries from couriers and royal mail where you are or will you incur extra charges for delivery? What is access like for larger vehicles or vehicles with trailers in case you are moving livestock or getting larger deliveries?

Living in a remote area is lovely, but when you realise you cannot buy items that aren't available locally easily, it can be frustrating and disturbing.

Location
The location of the smallholding is very important. Is it near to a hospital, which can be important as you grow older or if any of your family suffer from long-term health conditions. How far away are the shops? While it is great buying some shopping locally, travelling too far for a 'big' shop can be costly and time consuming, plus you need enough space in cupboards, fridges and freezers for storing the shopping.

Another consideration could be takeaway food. Living in a city, you get used to having a wide variety of takeaway food delivered or within easy driving distance. What takeaways are in the area of the smallholding and do any deliver to the property? Many families like to treat themselves to pizza or fish and chips once a week and it can be a bit of a culture shock to not be able to do that.

If you are planning on keeping livestock, then you need to know where you can take them to be slaughtered. Is there a local butcher or abattoir that can do this for you? You need to consider how far away they are and how you will transport the animals there.

House
What is the house like on the property? Is it big enough for your family? Does it have any restrictions on it such as Rural Occupancy? If the house is not big enough for your family, is there the space to extend it and can you afford to build an extension? Is the house in suitable condition for you to move in or

An Introduction to Smallholdings

does it need renovating? If it needs renovating, then both the cost and time has to be factored in to your plans as renovating the house is going to take time away from working on generating income. Also, can you live in the house while it is being renovated or do you need to live elsewhere in the meantime?

Outbuildings

Depending on what you are planning with your smallholding, you are going to need outbuildings of various sizes. At the very least, you will need somewhere to store tools and materials, but you may need somewhere to store vehicles and machinery. If you are keeping livestock, then you will need the appropriate buildings for them, which will vary depending on the number and type of livestock. They will need enough space to shelter from bad weather and stay indoors in winter, if necessary.

If the smallholding has these buildings, what condition are they in? Do they need work on or are they usable as is? If they are not on the smallholding, how much will it cost to build them and is there suitable access for vehicles and workmen? Some people convert outbuildings into holiday lets for an income. If this is part of your plan, are the buildings suitable for conversion and what are the estimated costs of conversion and running in utilities?

Outbuildings can also be converted into workshops and office lets, which can be a great source of income as many smaller companies love the idea of having their offices in a quiet, rural location.

An outbuilding that can be used as a workshop will be very helpful. In the colder, wetter months, you will appreciate an indoor space to do some work.

Also look at access to the outbuildings and how close they are to the main house. If you are keeping cattle, you don't really want them right next to the house due to the noise and smell.

Other Structures
Does the smallholding come with any other structures such as greenhouses and polytunnels? If it does, then this is a big money saver for you, though what condition are they in? Providing they are in good condition or easy to repair, then they are very helpful. Is there a shed or other storage facility in the garden area?

Utilities
Another consideration is what utilities, i.e. gas, electricity, water and sewage are on site? Smallholdings tend to be more remote than normal houses and this is not something that everyone thinks of. Running gas into a property that doesn't already have it can cost tens of thousands of pounds. Many smallholdings do not use gas for heating but have oil fired heating. This is more expensive than gas, requires a storage tank (which should be in place) and needs regular deliveries. You will need to factor the cost of oil into your budget and schedule deliveries regularly, though check access for the delivery vehicle.

Some smallholdings do not have mains sewage, but instead have a septic tank. This is something you need to be aware of because they require special care and there are some chemicals you cannot use in your house with a septic tank. They also require emptying regularly and, again, you need to ensure there is sufficient access for vehicles and factor the cost into your budget.

Almost all smallholdings will have water and electricity, though check the supply and any restrictions, particularly if your electricity supply can be intermittent in winter as this can impact your storage of food. It is possible to generate your own electricity from wind or solar energy and use geothermic energy for heating. However, there is a cost for these that you will need to factor into your budget. You will also need to find a suitable location for a wind turbine and the solar panels. The panels are often put on the roof of the house, but you need to check it can support them. If you have outbuildings and they are suitable, then the panels could always be put on those roofs instead. Be aware that if you are relying solely on generated electricity, then your usage patterns will need to change.

Another consideration is broadband connectivity. You and your family may be used to a fast broadband connection for online gaming and streaming video and TV shows. Moving to a smallholding and suddenly finding you cannot stream video or play games can be a major shock to the system and could be a deal breaker, particularly for children. While you can get satellite broadband, it is more expensive than regular broadband and nowhere near the same speed.

Your family may also want to consider mobile connectivity. Mobile connectivity is another consideration as many of us are reliant on our phones for communication. While it may be nice to have a break from your mobile phone, it can get frustrating to not be able to keep in contact with family and friends while being tied to a land line.

Local Market Conditions

As you need to generate an income from your smallholding, what is the local market like? Is there a big market for livestock and meat? Or do the locals like to buy fruit, vegetables and home-made produce? Perhaps the smallholding is near a tourist spot and glamping or holiday lets would be profitable. Investigating the local area and understanding what the market wants will help you determine how you can earn an income.

Your Priorities

There are a lot of decisions when choosing a smallholding and it is important that you know exactly what it is you want. Which features are essential and which are just nice to have. This will help you determine which smallholding is best for you. Decide the minimum size of land you want and the minimum size of house. Having these priorities will help you focus your search and get the property that you want.

Choosing a smallholding is a big decision and one that you will want to get right as moving after you get started involves a lot of disruption and effort. There is a lot to consider, but if you understand what features are necessities and which are just nice to have, then that will help you decide on the right property. Moving to a smallholding is a major life change and you need to ensure that you, and your family, are happy with the location you are moving to.

What To Grow On Your Smallholding

One of the main activities on any smallholding is growing fruits and vegetables. These are grown for you to eat in season and store for out of season use, but many smallholders grow some produce specifically to sell. Home-grown mushrooms, microgreens and salad greens sell very well to many restaurants that require fresh, good quality ingredients. Many other vegetables can be sold to vegetable box companies or even at a local farmer's market.

In your first year, you are going to be working hard getting the smallholding ready so you usually end up growing less than you would normally. Depending on when you move into the property, you may have missed the main growing season altogether and have to grow out of season plants or under cover. However, the advantage here is that you have time before the growing season to get the land ready for planting.

There will be good and bad years for vegetables, meaning one year you will get a glut of one type and the next you may struggle to grow them. Last year, I grew runner beans and had more beans than I could deal with. I ended up giving about 20kg to a food bank after I had filled my freezer and exhausted the good will of my friends and family. This year, I grew no runner beans. No matter what I did, they just would not germinate and grow.

You can mitigate against this by growing several varieties of each vegetable. This can ensure that at least some grow and produce a crop. If you discover that the area you live in suffers from particular plant diseases, look for disease resistant varieties so they have more of a chance to grow to maturity.

When growing to produce an income, you are looking for fast growing crops that quickly mature and can be sold. While plants such as purple sprouting broccoli does command a premium price, it takes up a lot of space and can take 10-11 months to mature depending on the variety. In the same space and time, you could get a lot of crops of lettuce, which, while it sells for a lower price, you can make more money because you have more harvests.

Another consideration is the quality of the soil on your smallholding. Hopefully, you have chosen a site with good soil, but if not, then you will need to improve it. Generally, most soils can be improved in a few years by working in plenty of well-rotted organic matter such as compost or manure. This will break up heavy soils and help free draining soils hold water better.

Starting plants off in a greenhouse or polytunnel will help to speed up the harvest and extend the growing season. Just remember to harden the plants off before planting out. Factor in all the expenses such as time, compost, tools, water, fuel, insurance and so on when calculating your pricing. Always invest in good quality tools as they last much longer than cheaper tools.

There are a lot of different things you can grow on your smallholding and you may decide to start with one or two of these suggestions and then expand your business as your skills improve and you get settled into the smallholding.

Organic vs Non-Organic

This is one of the big questions you need to consider as a smallholder. Are you going to farm, and sell, as organic or not?

For most small, market gardens selling direct, it just isn't worth well getting an organic certification as it takes time which can impact your earnings. It can take 2-3 years to get organic certification, during which time you cannot use certain chemicals and you cannot sell your produce as organic. However, there are grants available from the government to convert your land to organic farming.

While organic produce does command a premium, it does limit you in what you can and cannot use on your smallholding. It can also take some persuading to get customers to pay the premium price as many people still do not value organic produce.

It is important that you do not advertise your products as organic if you do not have the appropriate official certification as it is against the law and could get you into legal trouble. If you feel that growing organic is the way you want to go, then by all means acquire the certification.

Clearing The Land

Before you start anything, you will need to clear your land and prepare it for planting. While goats and sheep may appreciate scrubland, vegetable plants do not. Depending on the condition of your smallholding, this could be a substantial task and require heavy machinery.

Firstly, decide which areas are going to be for vegetable growing. These need to be as level as possible and have good quality soil. If the soil is heavy clay or too sandy, dig in plenty of organic matter every year until the soil improves. Many farmers will be happy to get rid of their manure and will often deliver it by the trailer load for a small fee. All you need to do is then transport it to your vegetable garden and dig it in. Fresh manure can be used providing you do not grow in it for 9-12 months to give it time to break down and finish rotting.

Clearing even a small piece of ground is hard work, particularly if it is overgrown or has difficult to remove roots in such as bramble or trees. It will be easier to use machinery such as a tractor or rotovator. If you do not have one, it may be worth buying one if you are going to use it often. Alternatively, they can be hired if you do not want to spend the money on buying the equipment.

Clear the stones out of the soil down to a spades depth and remove all the roots of perennial weeds like dandelion, dock and nettle. Turning the soil and then leaving it overnight will allow wildlife to clear pests from the soil.

It can also be worth investing in a high quality weed membrane to put over areas that you have dug or are not using. This will help to prevent weeds from growing back after you have spent the time digging. It also warms the soil and can allow for earlier planting in some areas. Some people plant through weed membrane to keep weeds down, which can reduce work weeding during the growing seasons.

Before planting any long term crops such as asparagus, rhubarb and perennial plants, make sure the soil is well dug, weeds and stones removed and organic matter dug in. These plants will be in place for 15-20 years, so it is important to prepare the soil properly to reduce the amount of work you have to do long term and keep the plants healthy.

Rather than try to tackle the whole smallholding, just work on an area at a time and then plant it or cover it. Taking on the whole site can be very overwhelming, whereas taking on an area at a time is much more manageable.

You may find it easier to mark out your vegetable beds and paths before you start and then you know exactly where you are digging and which areas you can leave grassed as pathways. Some people find having separate beds easier to manage than one big dug over area. It will help with crop rotation and allows you to target any soil improvements you are making.

Vegetables

Vegetables prefer a sunny, open location, so avoid areas that are too close to hedges, where the roots will compete for resources or overhanging trees which cast shade. Some vegetables, such as spinach, don't mind some shade and will grow well in the shadier areas of your smallholding.

Wherever you site your vegetable crop, place your compost heaps near to it. You do not want to be moving weeds or finished compost too far as it is extra work you don't need to be doing. Run in a water supply to near your vegetable beds for the same reason. Depending on the size of your vegetable plot, it may be beneficial to have multiple water sources to prevent you having to move water around. A long hose can make your life easier, though you have to be careful not to damage your plants by dragging the hose through them.

Greenhouses are really useful because they are a good environment for starting seedlings in and for growing half-hardy plants such as tomatoes, aubergines, peppers and chillies. Your greenhouse needs to be in an open location where it gets full sun all day. Do not site it near trees as falling branches can cause significant damage. Make sure it is not too exposed to the elements to try to protect it from the wind. Greenhouses need to be firmly fixed to the ground to prevent the wind from moving them or damaging them.

A polytunnel can also be useful for growing these half-hardy crops.

Polytunnels are cheaper than greenhouses, but they are more susceptible to wind damage. You need to be very careful to secure your polytunnel properly otherwise high winds will turn it into a kite and destroy your plants.

When growing vegetables, look at different varieties that mature at different times so you can avoid a glut and have a long harvest period. Cauliflowers, for example, can be ready any time from spring through to late autumn, depending on the variety. If you plant several different varieties, then you can be harvesting cauliflowers for many months, which means you can sell them for longer.

Another technique to extend the harvest is to use something known as succession planting. This is where instead of sowing an entire packet of radishes today, you sow one row today, another row in two weeks, another row two weeks later and so on. This means that instead of having an overwhelming number of radishes, you end up with a manageable amount regularly. This technique works for a variety of different crops and is a great way to have fresh vegetables throughout the growing season. If you are selling your produce, then you use succession planting on a larger scale so that you regularly have mature vegetables ready to harvest and sell. It saves you from having to store your produce which can cause you to lose some of your harvest and smooths out your income.

There are a lot of different crops you can grow and some you pick all at once, such as cauliflower where you remove the head. Others, such as kale, pak choi, lettuce and more are what are known as 'cut and come again' crops. This means that you harvest the outer leaves and leave the plant in place to grow more leaves. This can allow you to harvest the plant for several weeks or even longer and, again, you are not storing produce, but always using fresh vegetables.

From about October/November through to March/April time, you will find a lack of crops available to harvest. If you grow under cover, then some crops will grow in the colder months and some salad leaf crops will grow outside even in the dead of winter. Polytunnels and greenhouses will allow you to get some crops ready early in the season, which can certainly be an advantage if you are selling your produce.

An Introduction to Smallholdings

Some potential vegetable crops for a smallholding include:

- Asparagus
- Basil
- Beetroot
- Cabbage
- Cauliflower
- Celery
- Courgette
- Kale
- Lettuce
- Parsnip
- Physalis
- Radish
- Squash
- Tomatoes
- Winter salads
- Aubergine
- Beans (French, runner, broad)
- Broccoli
- Carrots
- Celeriac
- Chard
- Cucumber
- Leek
- Pak choi
- Peppers/chillies
- Onions
- Spinach
- Swede
- Turnip

There are all good crops to grow and can be profitable to sell. As said previously, grow several varieties of each one so that you can lengthen the harvesting period, which means you can sell more of them for longer.

Salad leaves and lettuces are a very good cash crop as no matter how big a grower you are, they still have to be harvested by hand. Growing some of these and selling them at farmer's markets, direct and to restaurants can be an excellent source of income. Restaurants in particular will be very interested in fresh salad, particularly if it can be delivered daily. Likewise, asparagus is another crop that earns good money, but it takes up a lot of space in a permanent bed, takes 2-3 years before it is fully productive and is only harvested for 2-3 months a year.

Steady sources of income come from crops that do not require a great deal of involvement from you such as beetroot, beans, courgettes, squashes and so on. Pumpkins take up a lot of space, but can be a good cash crop in October for Hallowe'en. Most root crops are also good earners and good to sell into vegetable box companies. You could, if you can grow enough, start your own local vegetable box!

Fruit

Fruit is another popular crop on smallholdings both as a source of income and as something for the family. Fruit takes a lot of work up front to get the ground prepared and the plants in, but you will get a long term harvest from them. Fruit trees can take several years before they are productive and longer before they fully mature. Fruit bushes can take 2-4 years to produce fully, but once they do, fruit is a relatively passive source of food and income.

Basic maintenance on fruit is quite low. There is a little bit of pruning each year at the right time and some feeding. Apart from that, there is little else for you to do! Some trees need grease bands applying in winter to protect them from codling moths while others benefit from spraying for pests, but apart from that, there isn't a great deal to do.

Apples, plums and pears are staple fruit trees in the UK, though depending on where you are located, you may also be able to grow peaches, nectarines, apricots and even pomegranates. Greengages are a delicious crop, but one that seems to have fallen out of favour.

There are plenty of fruit bushes you can grow from blackcurrants to blackberries to gooseberries and raspberries. Again, these are popular and have to be picked by hand. Some, such as gooseberries, you do not tend to find in the shops, so they can sell well to people that like them but do not grow them at home.

When planting fruit trees, you need to consider the maximum height the trees will grow. Full sized trees will grow very high, which can make harvesting difficult. Look for dwarf or semi-dwarf rootstock. The mature trees are smaller and much easier to harvest from. If you really want an easy harvest, look at training your trees along wires as espaliers. A dwarf fruit tree also has the advantage of producing fruit much quicker than full sized apple trees, meaning you could start to see fruit in the second year.

Another advantage of dwarf trees is that you can fit more into the land you have, and they sit quite well in areas that would otherwise be difficult to use.

The key for success with fruit trees is to ensure that you have trees that flower around the same time. Apple trees in particular, flower at different times and if you do not have multiple trees in flower at the same time, then pollination will not happen. It is worth having a crab apple tree or two on your property too because these will pollinate all apple trees. Crab apples make good hedging trees.

Fruit bushes are very easy to grow and will produce a good harvest. Blackcurrants are popular made into jam (they work well with apple), pies, cordial or sold as is. Raspberries are great by themselves or made into a jam, but harvest them regularly as they will very quickly become too ripe. Blackberries are brilliant, particularly if you buy thornless cultivars that produce large berries. These are expensive to buy in the stores and are very popular with a lot of people.

If you want to grow something more unusual, then blueberries grow well in this country, but they require an acidic soil to produce a good crop. Goji berries, also known as wolf berries, are a popular superfood that you could also grow and sell or make into something such as granola bars.

There are many other types of berries, but these would typically be grown for your own use because they are not generally known or used by most people.

For yourselves, you can turn your fruit into jams, cordials, fruit leathers, fruit butters and more. It can be stewed and frozen, or just frozen whole in the case of berries. Apples and pears will, when stored correctly, stay good for several months and into the following year.

For selling, fruit needs to be very carefully handled because a lot of it is very easily damaged, which then makes it harder to sell. You can make more income from the fruit by turning it into something. Home-made pies, jams and cakes are very popular and will command a premium price. They also last longer and are generally easier to transport than the fruit itself.

Fruit is an important part of your diet and home-grown fruit is a wonderful treat throughout the year, particularly when made into pies or jams. There is a lot you can do with fruit and you need to consider which fruits to grow on your smallholding. Don't forget that there are fruits in the wild that may already be growing on your smallholding such as sloe, damson and elder. While these may not be commercially viable, you can certainly make wine, jam and cordial out of them for your own use. An elderberry cordial is a wonderful winter tonic that boosts your immune system to protect you from winter bugs.

Herbs

Herbs are another important part of a smallholding and are good not only in your kitchen, but they are a very good commercial crops. Restaurants like to buy fresh herbs and they can be popular on market stalls too. Starting a herb garden does not require a lot of investment as many can be started from seed. Remember that invasive weeds such as mints and lemon balm should be grown in containers otherwise they will rapidly take over an area.

Most herbs will grow happily outside in the British climate, but some Mediterranean herbs such as basil, prefer a warmer environment and benefit from being under cover during the cooler months.

Herbs lend themselves very well to hydroponic growing, which we will discuss shortly. They are typically ready to harvest quicker and many people claim they have more flavour when grown without soil.

If you are planning on selling the herbs, then it doesn't matter where the herb garden is sited, providing each herb can have the conditions that it prefers. Herbs for your own use are best grown near to your kitchen so you can grab them easily while cooking. They lend themselves nicely to being grown in containers or in a vertical garden.

Herbs can be sold in many different ways such as:

- Fresh plants
- Bagged fresh herbs
- Dried herbs
- Dried herb mixes

Or they can be made into products and sold, such as:

- Teas
- Candles

- Bath products
- Beauty products

There are a lot of different herbs that you can grow. Some of the more profitable and popular herbs are:

- Basil
- Chamomile
- Coriander
- Lavender
- Oregano
- Rosemary
- Tarragon (French)
- Catnip
- Chives
- Dill
- Marjoram
- Parsley
- Sage

Herbs have another benefit for your smallholding in that many will repel pests and are excellent companion plants for fruits and vegetables. Some, such as marjoram and lavender produce copious amounts of flowers which attract pollinating insects. This is hugely advantageous to you because they will also pollinate your fruit and vegetable crops.

If you can, having plants on site that flower from early in the season to late on, then this will help ensure you get a good crop. It is important, as a smallholder, that you encourage pollinating insects onto your land so that they can pollinate your crops.

Mushrooms

Many smallholders do not think about growing mushrooms, yet they can be a very profitable crop. There is a big demand for fresh mushrooms, particularly for oriental and specialty mushrooms such as oyster, though normal button or chestnut mushrooms can be popular too.

The nice thing with mushrooms is that they can be grown vertically, so you can get high yields from a small area. One room will house enough mushrooms to earn a decent income. An outbuilding on your smallholding could be converted into space for growing mushrooms.

Mushrooms grow rapidly so you can get multiple harvests every year. Although they can require more work than other crops to get them started, they are fairly self-sufficient once established.

In 2017-2018 in the USA, the speciality mushroom market was worth over $106 million, with start-up costs being low. Many mushrooms will also grow outside with spores being planted on cut logs. If you are growing indoors, you will need lighting and temperature control as you need to mimic the outdoor conditions the mushrooms are used to.

Mushrooms can be sold fresh or dried and sold. Again, restaurants and markets are good places to sell your crop. Speciality shops could also be interested in stocking dried mushrooms as they have a longer shelf life. Some vegetable box schemes may also buy mushrooms for the boxes.

Garlic

Garlic is a very profitable crop and one that is very easy to grow and low maintenance. It is an excellent market to be in with garlic being sold direct, through vegetable box schemes and when processed, such as pickled and preserved. One rapidly growing, profitable market is that of Black Garlic, which is popular in Korean dishes. Smoked garlic is another popular way of processing this crop for sale, for which you will need a smoker.

One of the big advantages of garlic is that it is an excellent winter crop, making use of ground that would otherwise not be planted. It is typically planted around November and harvested in June. Traditionally, garlic is planted on the shortest day and harvested on the longest, but most people plant a bit earlier these days. Garlic requires cold in order for the bulbs to split and form cloves. Onions and shallots are another good over-winter crop, being planted at the same time as garlic. You just need to be aware that the beds garlic is in will not be usable until the end of June. It is possible to start off some plants in the garlic beds before harvest time, but you have to be careful not to damage either plant.

Once planted, which is very easy to do, garlic needs very little care. This crop does not like competition, so you need to keep the weeds down. A quick visit with your hoe once or twice a week is usually enough. It does not require a great deal of watering. As winters tend to be quite wet in this country, you usually only have to water them a couple of times a week in dry spells.

There are a lot of different types of garlic, so you should investigate whether to grow hardneck, softneck or even the milder elephant garlic, which is more expensive to buy. They do have slightly different requirements and cope with different environmental conditions.

The nice thing about garlic is there is an initial expense in buying the cloves to plant, but once you have your first harvest, you can put aside cloves to plant next season, which saves you some money.

Garlic is certainly a good crop for any smallholder to grow because it is low maintenance and grows at a time when not a lot else does. It is relatively tolerant of different soil types and so long as you keep the weeds down, it will produce a good crop year after year.

Microgreens

Microgreens have become very popular in recent years because they are considered a delicacy and to be very good for you. Microgreens are plants that are bigger than a sprout, but not quite a baby plant. Sprouts are also another potentially profitable crop, particularly if you live in an area that is very health conscious.

The advantage of microgreens is that they have a lot of flavour, are very nutritious and only take 2-3 weeks to grow! This means that you have a very good turnover of produce and a constant crop, which is important as they have a short shelf life and restaurants in particular will need regular deliveries.

Microgreens are grown indoors and they do not require a great deal of space to get started. You can grow them in any room or your greenhouse. This is an excellent crop to grow over winter while there is not a great deal you can grow outside, so can be a good source of income.

This crop can be sold direct to customers, at farmer's markets or to restaurants. They are popular as a garnish or ingredient with restaurants. High-end restaurants in particularly are very keen on fresh microgreens.

Aquaponics

Aquaponics is a modern technique that is very interesting. It is a method mixing hydroponics (growing without soil) with aquaculture, keeping fish. It combines these two growing techniques to produce both plants and fish. The initial start-up costs can be high, but it can be very productive and provide two sources of income.

This growing technique dates back thousands of years. In ancient China, carp and eels were farmed in rice paddy fields. Aquaponics works because the fish produce waste that bacteria in the water convert to nitrites, which the plants feed on. It is a very clever system that can be scaled to whatever level you want, and allows you to benefit from two very different income sources from one setup. Plus, it can be used to give your family fresh fish too.

An aquaponics system consists of:

- A rearing tank that the fish are kept in
- A settling basin that captures and filters out uneaten fish food
- A biofilter containing bacteria that converts the fish waste into nitrites
- A hydroponic system to grow the plants in
- A sump which pumps the water around

An aquaponics system can be used to farm ornamental fish to sell as pets or a variety of different fish for eating. There are a lot of different types of fish you can use in an aquaponics system, including:

- Tilapia – not a popular fish in the UK, but edible and tolerates a wide range of conditions
- Trout – edible, but grow slowly, though tolerant of cooler temperatures. They taste good and are a popular eating fish preferring a carnivorous diet themselves
- Catfish – a hardy, edible fish that is easy to raise
- Largemouth Bass – popular eating fish that is tolerant of a wide variety of water conditions
- Salmon – a very popular eating fish, though needs a large tank and will take two years before they are ready for harvesting
- Koi – ornamental fish that has a high value when sold
- Fancy goldfish – an ornamental fish that is very easy to keep
- Ornamental fish such as guppies, mollies, angelfish and tetras

- Murray Cod – a hungry fish that grows fast, but is edible
- Prawns/shrimp – fast growing, popular as an edible crop, but will be eaten if kept with other fish

This is a good system to use that allows to you to grow vegetables and herbs, which benefit from being grown in hydroponics, and combine it with fish, which can be an excellent source of food and income. It does require some specialist knowledge, which is not hard to acquire and requires some work monitoring the temperature and pH of the system. However, it is rewarding and could potentially be a good source of income for your smallholding.

Hydroponics

Hydroponics is pretty much the same as aquaponics but without the fish! Rather than the fish providing the nutrients, you add it manually to the water. This method of growing without soil has a lot of advantages in that the plants grow faster and many people feel they taste better too.

The disadvantage is the setup costs are high and the fact, like aquaponics, you must have a stable electricity supply to keep the water circulating. However, there are plenty of advantages to this method of growing, not least of which is you don't have to do any digging and you are not reliant on the British weather.

Again, this is a very clever way of growing plants that does not depend on the weather. It allows for high yields as it is possible to grow a lot of plants in a small area because you can grow vertically in hydroponic towers.

Being able to grow herbs and vegetables such as cucumber, strawberries and tomatoes all year round puts you in an advantageous position as a business because you are able to supply local restaurants with fresh produce out of season. Typically, a hydroponic crop is ready anywhere between 20-40% faster than one growing using traditional methods. Because of the way they are grown, they tend to have a lot of flavour and a good, uniform look.

This is certainly something to look into as it can be a very good way to grow fresh produce all year round to sell and use yourself. The start-up costs are high and you will need to understand how hydroponics works, but it is a great, high tech way to grow vegetables.

Christmas Tree Farm

If you have some land that you are not using or is not suitable for crops, then setting up a Christmas tree farm could be a really good idea! The downside of a Christmas tree farm is that it will take 6-10 years from planting until the trees are ready to harvest.

During this time, you will need to care for the trees shape them and prune them. You start with a single, upright leader and once the trees have reached 4-7 feet tall (depending on how tall you want them to grow), you cut the top off the tree every summer so the branches thicken and they form the traditional shape of a Christmas tree.

Growing Christmas trees isn't a lot of work and you can sell the trees as living trees in pots, which are popular, or you can cut the trees down for people. Alternatively, people can harvest their own tree, which some people really enjoy and it takes some of the work away from you.

Christmas trees are a very seasonal crop, but they are a good way of making use of land that isn't suitable for any other use. As well as selling trees, you can also grow and sell holly, make wreaths and more, all of which will go well with the Christmas tree. As well as this, you could sell home-made produce such as jams and chutneys as these are always popular for Christmas.

Some of the popular Christmas trees including Douglas fir, blue spruce and balsam fir. While you are waiting for the crop to mature, keep planting new plants every year so that there is a harvest every year. People like good quality Christmas trees, and it can be a good way to earn some income while engaging with the local community.

Profit margins are quite high on Christmas trees and around 1,500 can be grown in one acre. Most trees will produce new seedlings, which you can then re-plant for a future crop, which is a good money saver.

If you have some land that you are not using or is not suitable for agriculture, then a Christmas tree farm is a good investment. It does require money up front to pay for the saplings, but the land wasn't going to otherwise make any money. After a few years, once you build up a reputation for supplying Christmas trees, it can turn into a very lucrative business and ancillary services could be offered such as Santa's grotto, decorations, cards and more.

Crop Rotation For Smallholders

One subject that needs to be addressed is that of crop rotation. This is very important for the health of your plants and soil, being the principle of not growing the same crops in the same piece of ground year after year. If you do, then you are encouraging the build-up of harmful pests and diseases in the soil which can wreck your crops. Rotating your crops between plots means planting in fresh soil and that many potentially serious problems never get a chance to get established. As a smallholder, reliant on the land, healthy soil is of the upmost importance so it is important you rotate your crops so you get the best harvest possible and keep pests and diseases to a minimum.

A big part of companion planting is to interplant one crop with another. For example, in crop rotation, you wouldn't grow garlic in the same bed two years in a row. However, with companion planting, you may plant the odd garlic bulb in between many of your other plants.

You may then think you can't grow garlic again in those areas, even as a companion plant. However, as you are only growing a small amount of garlic, you are very unlikely to suffer from a build-up of pathogens in the soil. Therefore, when companion planting individual or small amounts of plants, crop rotation can go out of the window. It is okay to plant companions in the same spots year after year, though if you do notice any consistent problems or suffer from any diseases, you will have to move them.

For those growing larger amounts of vegetables, crop rotation is very important. You need to move crops every year so that they are not always being grown in the same place. The smallholder will have to practice crop rotation every year. Always keep a written record of what you have planted where so that you can rotate your crops correctly. Anyone planting in rows, blocks or filling raised beds with one or two plants will need to practice crop rotation to reduce potential problems.

Some perennial crops such as strawberries, rhubarb and asparagus do not fit into any crop rotation plan as they are permanent crops. You are not going to dig up any of these and move them every year; you would never get a crop. These are planted in one place for their lifetime, with the soil being conditioned every year to keep it nutritious and healthy.

Some annual crops such as French and runner beans, sweet corn, and salad crops can be grown pretty much anywhere, though try to avoid growing them too often in the same place. Other crops like pumpkins, courgettes, squashes, potatoes, tomatoes, carrots, onions, and all members of the brassica family need to be rotated every year because pests and diseases can build up in the soil.

Blight, for example, which affects tomatoes and potatoes can overwinter in the soil, particularly if diseased foliage is accidentally dug in or diseased potatoes are left in the ground, which always happens. Moving the crop the following year means the disease can die off and will not be able to immediately re-infect your crop.

Crop rotation is usually planned over winter before you start planting anything out. That gives you time to prepare the soil, if necessary, and mark out beds where necessary.

Crop rotation has a lot of benefits for you, the smallholder, including:

- Improves soil fertility – rotating crops prevents one particular vegetable from exhausting the soil of nutrients. Done properly, it allows you to build up nutrient levels in the soil, such as planting beans and digging in the roots to fix nitrogen.
- Weed control – planting squashes and potatoes provides a lot of ground cover, which helps to suppress weeds and prevent the problems associated with them.
- Pest/disease control – as soil borne pests and diseases tend to target a specific family of plants, you can prevent this damage simply by not growing the same vegetable in the same place for three to four years. In this time, the pest or disease should have died off and won't be a problem when you re-introduce the original vegetable back to that bed. Crop rotation is used to avoid a variety of diseases such as white rot in onions and club root in brassicas.

Rotating Your Crops

You can make crop rotation as simple or as complex as you want. I tend to keep it on the simple side because I find it much easier to keep track of. Your plants are grouped into five groups, excluding perennial plants such as rhubarb and asparagus.

1. Brassicas – Brussels sprouts, cabbage, cauliflower, kale, kohlrabi, oriental greens (including chards), radish, swede, and turnips (rutabaga)
2. Legumes – broad beans and peas (both French and runner beans have fewer problems with soil-borne diseases and can be planted anywhere)
3. Onions – garlic, leek, onion, and shallot
4. Potato family – potato, and tomato (although peppers and aubergines are in the same family, they have fewer problems and can be grown anywhere except when an area suffers from blight and then you will want to include them in your crop rotation scheme)
5. Root crops – beetroot, carrot, celeriac, celery, fennel (though this doesn't get on with most plants so is planted towards the edge of most vegetable gardens), parsley, parsnip, and any other root crop.

Each year you simply move each section of your vegetable garden one step forward, so the bed that contained legumes will have brassicas in the following year. Let me give you a very simple, three-year crop rotation plan based on the majority of crops being brassicas and potatoes:

First Year
Bed One – Potatoes
Bed Two – Legumes, onions, and root crops
Bed Three – Brassicas

Second Year
Bed One – Legumes, onions, and root crops
Bed Two – Brassicas
Bed Three – Potatoes

Year Three
Bed One – Brassicas
Bed Two – Potatoes
Bed Three – Legumes, onions, and root crops

The same principles apply when performing a four-year crop rotation plan. Depending on the size of your vegetable garden you may work on either a three or four-year schedule. Smaller areas work well on a three-year rotation plan, whereas larger areas benefit from a four-year rotation plan.

In my crop rotation plan, I have one or two beds that are devoted to onions or shallots as I use a lot of them. I have another bed dedicated to garlic. These form part of my crop rotation plan. However, I also plant some onions near to my brassicas as part of my companion planting, and usually, some kohlrabi makes its way into my onion bed for the same reason. As the brassicas are rotated every year, so the onions are also rotated every year, keeping to the principles of crop rotation.

This works and is fine; you can do the same. However, if I were to see any evidence of white rot or other problems in the onions, I would avoid planting any onions, even as companion plants, in that bed for several years.

Crop rotation is an important tool in natural, organic gardening and will help minimize diseases and pests in your garden. A well thought out crop rotation plan nicely compliments your companion planting, helping to reduce your reliance on chemicals as you naturally control the pests on your vegetable plot.

Keeping Livestock

Most smallholders will keep some form of livestock. Whether this is a few chickens for fresh eggs or cows, pigs, llamas, alpacas, ostriches or sheep is up to you and will depend on the size of your land and which animals you want to keep.

Animals are either kept for meat for your family or they are kept and sold for profit. Animals are a good source of fertilizer for your crops, and they do require a lot of work. You will be tied to your smallholding as it is much harder to go on holiday when you are looking after various animals. They often require work at anti-social hours and need you to step outside of your comfort zone, particularly if you have to milk cattle or help them give birth.

You will need enough space for the animals and ensure that you do not overcrowd them. As well as outdoor space, which must be properly fenced to prevent them from escaping or damaging other parts of your smallholding, they need indoor space. Depending on the animal, they may need to be brought inside at night, during bad weather or in winter.

When keeping animals for meat, you either have to decide to butcher them yourself or send them away to be butchered for you. Most people are not comfortable slaughtering animals themselves, so it is easier to send the animals away. Butchering animals is a specialist skill that needs to be done correctly and there are only certain animals you are allowed to slaughter on your smallholding. Just make sure you do not get too attached to the animals as it makes it much harder to send the animals to slaughter. If you have children, be careful they do not get attached to the meat animals as it can be traumatic for them to see their 'pets' disappear.

Some of the popular animals kept on smallholdings include:

- Cows – good for milk and meat, though you will need milking equipment unless doing it by hand
- Sheep – can be milked, though usually kept for wool and meat
- Goats – can be milked, but usually kept for meat or as general waste disposal (they eat virtually anything). Pygmy goats can be very popular with children
- Pigs – kept for meat and popular with smallholders as a source of bacon and sausages
- Llamas – make for good guard 'dogs' and can protect your herds from predators
- Alpaca – kept for wool which commands a good price or can be made into clothing
- Chickens – most smallholders own at least a few chickens. They are kept for eggs and meat. Some people keep quail as the eggs are worth more
- Rabbits – more commonly kept as pets, but can be kept for meat, but are an acquired taste
- Deer – a less common livestock, but can be kept for meat

Which livestock you choose to keep is entirely up to you, but be careful you don't bite off more than you can chew. Livestock is a significant commitment and you need to full understand all the implications about owning the animals from caring to them to their purpose on your smallholding to looking after them when they are ill or birthing.

It would be a good idea that your family learn about the animals too and help you look after them so that if you are unwell, the animals are well cared for.

Remember to factor in the cost of the animals as well as their 'running costs' such as feed, insurances, vaccinations, medical treatment and so on.

If you are planning on selling the meat you produce, then check what you can and cannot sell. Meat is a very controlled market and it needs to be handled, stored and labelled correctly, particularly if you are selling beef. If you are selling at farmer's markets, there are very strict rules about what you can and cannot sell, so you need to familiarise yourself with them.

Chickens

Chickens are ideal for a smallholder to start with as the start-up costs are low, they are relatively easy to look after and they do not need a lot of resources.

Hens themselves are quite cheap, with ex-battery hens costing no more than a couple of pounds. These hens usually have a few years of laying left in them and then can be kept as pets or used in the cooking pot.

Pure breed hens are more expensive and can cost anywhere from £10-£20 or more per bird, depending on the breed. Some breeds are good layers, some are good meat birds and others are good at both. It depends on what you want your chickens for as to which breed you get, but some of them are very pretty to look at. Just be careful that you do not buy an aggressive breed and mix it in with a more timid breed as they can end up fighting.

Hens will nest in a hen house or an outhouse, so long as it is secure from foxes. Hens will happily roam free and will eat weeds, slugs and other insects. Be aware that they will also eat your seedlings and other plants you are growing, so keep them away from your vegetable garden.

How many eggs a chicken lays will depend on the breed and the weather, as some breeds are more prolific layers than others. Typically, you will get one egg every 1-2 days, depending on the breed. During colder months, chickens lay fewer eggs than they do in the summer months.

You can buy day old chicks, which are very cute and adorable. The only trouble is that it can be hard to determine which are male and which are the females you want. Then you have to get rid of the male birds. It will take up to 18 weeks for hens to start laying, or you can buy young chickens at laying age if you prefer.

Hens are usually not slaughtered until they are a year old as after this time, egg production can slow. If you are raising chickens from eggs, then you will know that male hens are not generally wanted, so these are usually fattened up and slaughtered or killed as soon as they are sexed.

Grass fed chickens produce meet and eggs that taste much better than that from factory farmed birds. Make sure your chickens are properly vaccinated and you should not need to treat them with antibiotics.

Excess eggs can be sold either at farmer's markets with your vegetables, to restaurants or directly.

Some of the popular chicken breeds for smallholders include:

- Araucana – a hardy chicken that looks very nice and produces blue shelled eggs. Keep them separate from other chickens as they can be bullied as their combs block their eyesight
- Leghorn – produces plenty of white eggs
- Marans – produce dark brown eggs and can be good meat birds
- Orpington – a very fluffy breed that does not like to get wet and needs a lot of space, being a large bird. Good layers and good for eating too
- Rhode Island Red – lays large, brown eggs, is good at foraging and is a hardy bird
- Sussex – a good dual purpose breed that is good at foraging and is a good choice for new keepers
- Wyandotte – very calm bird that likes being handled. Lays around 200 eggs a year, though it can become broody

As well as chickens, some smallholders keep ducks, geese, quail or even turkeys. The latter are typically only kept for their meat, but ducks, quail and geese are also kept for eggs, which can be sold. If you are keeping ducks or geese, then you need a body of water for them.

All birds will need their wings clipping each year to prevent them from flying off. While chickens in particular are not good fliers, they can fly enough to get over a fence and escape. You can build runs for them, or you can clip their wings and allow them to roam on your smallholding.

Chickens are probably a good type of livestock to start with because they do not take up a lot of space, are easy to keep and will earn their keep through eggs. A flock of 6-10 birds will easily provide enough eggs each week for most families without being a great burden to look after.

Micro-Dairy

If you have sufficient space, then you can set up your own micro-diary, which is a small scale dairy farm. You will need at least four cows, milking equipment, a cow shed and enough space for the cows to roam and feed.

The milk can be sold as locally grown milk or it can be processed into butter, cream, yoghurt or other dairy products, which you can also sell.

There is a definite shift in consumer buying habits, where people are much more interested in buying locally sourced products and they don't mind paying a premium for them.

Running a dairy farm takes some work, but it can be scaled up slowly as demand increased. While you may not be able to compete with large scale dairy farms on price, selling locally can be profitable for you.

It may be difficult to turn dairy farming into a full time income, but it can be a good alternative source of income as well as provide for the needs of your family.

Meat Farming

Meat farming can be anything from keeping a couple of animals to provide most of your meat needs for the year, to keeping extra animals to sell the meat.

Sheep, cows, pigs and even goats are popular for meat, as are chickens. Meat from a small scale farm, such as your smallholding typically has much more flavour than that from large scale operations and is more nutritious. Firstly, it doesn't usually have the antibiotics in it that can be found in commercially produced meat, but also being raised on pasture makes a big difference to taste.

Before you think about selling meat, be aware that there are a rules and regulations for the handling, packaging, slaughtering and storage of meat which you must adhere to. Before you buy your first animals, make sure you are familiar with these if you are planning on selling any meat. If you are keeping it for your own family, then you do not need to know this information, particularly if you are not planning on slaughtering the animals yourself.

Next, decide what type of animals you want to keep and then look for a local butcher or abattoir that can slaughter your animals for you. You will need to think about how the animals will be transported there and any costs involved.

Raising animals requires a lot of knowledge and you should invest in some books and even some training courses to learn how to look after the animals properly. It is very important that you how to do this for the animal's welfare and to follow the required rules and regulations.

Animals require a good amount of space as well as specialist equipment such as waterers, fencing, pens, trailers (for transportation) and more. The larger the animal, the more it will eat, so factor these costs into your budget as well as an amount for vet fees and vaccinations.

It is also worth considering insurance for your animals. You will need third party liability insurance in case your animals escape and cause damage, plus you can insure your animals if they are part of your business.

Pigs

Pigs are a good animal to keep as they will eat almost anything and produce a wide variety of popular meats, most of which can easily be sold if required. Depending on where you live, you may get inspected to ensure you have a suitable environment for them. If you are planning on selling meat, then you will need a Country Parish Holding and a herd number, plus you will not be allowed to feed the pigs on anything from your home.

A mature pig can produce around 1000lbs of meat, which can keep your family in meat for a long time. It is illegal to slaughter a pig at home yourself, so you will need to arrange to transport the animals to a butcher.

Pigs can live outside most of the time, but benefit from being able to go indoors when they want. You will need strong fencing around their pen as some breeds can grow quite big and can damage weaker fencing.

Some popular pig breeds for the smallholder include:

- Berkshire – a traditional pork pig that produces particularly good crackling
- Hampshire – produces lean meat
- Landrace – a lean breed that grows rapidly and produces plenty of bacon

- Oxford Sandy or Black – a good pig for beginners as it is quite docile and produces plenty of good quality port and bacon
- Large White – produce good quality, lean milk
- Welsh – a hardy breed that produces very good ham

Cows

Cows can be kept on the smallholding and are probably the most demanding animals to keep. There is a lot of paperwork involved in keeping cows as well as physical work. Be prepared to be up at dawn every day to milk the cows and to raise calves yourself or send them for slaughter. A single cow can produce enough milk for 2-3 people in a year, plus the manure makes for excellent fertiliser for your vegetable garden.

Cows require good outdoor space to roam and feed, as well as indoor space to shelter from the weather. You should have strong fencing to keep them in. They are often kept indoors over winter and you will need to provide them with food during this time.

Some popular cow breeds for smallholders include:

- Aberdeen Angus – an excellent beef cow that produces very high quality meat
- Ayrshire – a very good, hardy milk cow
- British White – a large cow that produces plenty of milk and a lot of beef
- Dexter – about half the size of a Hereford, weighing on average 300-350kg. Good for both milk and beef
- Hereford – compact, beefy animal weighing 500-600kg. They live a long time and are easy to calf. Each cow will produce between 250-350kg of beef and are ready to slaughter from about 30 months
- Highland – calves until around 20 years old and produces good quality, low fat beef

Sheep

Sheep are a popular animal on smallholdings because they take up less space than cows, and they are great lawn mowers. Cows prefer longer grass, whereas sheep are happier with shorter grass, such as that left behind by grazing cows. Goats are similar to sheep, but are voracious eaters and will lay waste to your vegetable garden if given half a chance.

Both sheep and goats are a good source of milk, though it is more of an acquired taste than cow's milk. Sheep are good for wool, and both animals can be eaten, but goat is, again, an acquired taste. Some people keep pygmy goats for the children as they are cute and sociable animals.

Sheep need a good fenced pasture and indoor space to shelter, though generally they do not like being indoors. Your fencing needs to be robust as sheep are excellent escape artists. Be prepared to help them with lambing in the spring and that sheep do seem to get ill quite often. They will need shearing each year, which you can either learn to do yourself or hire someone to do it for you. The wool can be used in your home or sold.

There are two types of sheep:

1. Highland Sheep – smaller, hardy, have one lamb a year which takes 18 months to mature for slaughter, happy to live on the side of a mountain
2. Lowland Sheep – easier to tame, often have multiple lambs that mature in around 6 months, does not like mountains and needs lush meadows

Of each of these, there are many different breeds, with some breeds being better for milk and others better for producing wool.

Some popular sheep breeds for the smallholder include:

- East Friesian – large, excellent dairy sheep with a medium grade wool, but not very hardy
- Merino – a medium sized sheep, that breeds well and is hardy. It produces high grade wool and is good for showing
- Polypay – large sheep that are good for meat and produce a good

grade wool, plus it is quite hardy
- Suffolk – a very large sheep that breeds well with a medium quality wool. It is mainly kept for its meat, but is also good for showing

Of course, there are many unusual or primitive breeds that you can buy for your smallholding if you prefer something a little bit more unusual. Do your research and decide which breed best suits your needs as it is no good buying a sheep for wool that produces poor quality wool!

You will need to have a County Parish Holding Number before you keep sheep and, if you want to breed your sheep, a flock number from your local Animal Health Section, which is a part of your local authority Environmental Department.

Typically, you allow five sheep per acre so they have enough space for grazing. Sheep have a reputation for getting themselves into trouble, so you will want to check them a couple of times a day to make sure they aren't stuck in a hedge or on their backs (it happens more often than you may think).

It is worth attending a course and learning more about keeping sheep if you are planning on having them on your smallholding. They can need their feet trimming a couple of times a year and lambing is a particular skill you will have to learn, but they are a good animal to have.

Beekeeping

Another type of animal to keep on your smallholding are bees. These are very useful as pollinators for your plants, but they also produce honey and other products which can be worth selling. Bee products are very popular and can be sold as is or made into beauty products to sell. As pollinators, they will help to increase your yields and ensure you get fruit from your trees.

You will need to attend a beekeeping course to learn how to keep bees. It is not something simple to do, but it is a lot of fun. How many hives you have will depend on your space and how much time you want to commit, but it is well worth keeping at least one or two hives to supply your family with honey for the year.

Bee hives can sit on land that is not good for growing vegetables or grazing animals. Ideally, they need a quiet corner of your smallholding, away from neighbours and your house.

You will need to plant to encourage bees, so ensure there are flowers from early in the year through the late autumn. Planting flowering herbs such as lavender and marjoram will help a lot, particularly if you plant them around your fruit trees to encourage the bees to pollinate them. Dandelions are an important early season food for bees, though once the flowers are finished, remove the heads and dispose of them.

It doesn't cost a lot to get started keeping bees, you will need a couple of hives, bee suits and some equipment, plus honey extractors too. It isn't a full time job to look after these helpful creatures and it is fascinating watching the bees go about their business.

Bees provide you with beeswax, which can be made into soap, candles and other beauty products. Royal jelly, propolis and bee pollen are considered superfoods and command a premium price,

Bees will require more time in the summer months than in winter, when they pretty much go dormant and just require occasionally checking. They are a good addition to any smallholding and local honey always sells for a premium price. The products you can make from the bees can help attract people to your market stall and bring in additional income, particularly in the winter months when there may not be so many vegetables to sell.

Snail Farming

Heliciculture is snail farming, and not something you probably ever thought about doing on your smallholding. Snails are more often considered a pest than a delicious snack! However, although snails are not that popular in the UK, there is still a good market for escargot plus they are popular on the continent. At present, they are gaining in popularity with high-end restaurants which like fresh, good quality, local ingredients.

Snails are hermaphrodites, so they can choose to be male or female, which makes breeding extremely easy. They need very little help from you, just an environment that is suitable for them.

A snail farm consists of special garden beds that are edged with a very tight mesh fence that the snails cannot get through or over. The snails are fed leafy green plants, which gives them a much 'smoother' taste and acts as their home.

For each square metre of space, you can fit about 1kg of snails, though if you pack them too densely, they will not breed well.

Snail farming is not something that people automatically think of when it comes to smallholding, but it could be a good, additional source of income, especially if you are already selling herbs and microgreens into high-end restaurants. They are fairly easy to look after, do not require a great deal of space and command a good price for what they are.

There are a lot of different animals that you can keep on your smallholding, and which you do will depend on where your smallholding is located and the type of animals you want to keep. You need to make sure that the animals you are planning on keeping will be okay in your area.

If you are living in the depths of Scotland where it is cold in winter, keeping animals that prefer warmer climates is not going to work. It will be a lot of work and expense to ensure these animals are comfortable during the colder months. However, with most animals, there are some breeds that like warmer weather and some that prefer colder, so you can usually find something that will be suitable for where you will be living.

Livestock is an important part of being a smallholder, but make sure you get the animals you are comfortable. If you are not happy about raising animals and sending them off to slaughter, then perhaps just keep a few chickens for eggs and maybe a single cow for milk. Research the various animals and determine which are the best for your needs and goals as a smallholder.

Reducing Your Environmental Impact

Environmental issues are a major concern for us all at present and one that, as a smallholder, you should also consider. Becoming more eco-friendly is typically one of the issues that cause people to move to a smallholding. So how do you reduce your environmental impact?

There are many things you can do such as creating a haven for wildlife, designed with birds and bugs in mind, or planting an awesome flower garden to feed bees or a vegetable garden with no chemicals or plastics in sight. There is so much you can do to reduce your environmental impact. Creating an eco-friendly garden does not mean you have to limited in what you can do ... it just means you do it in a way which is in harmony with nature.

So what can you do to create the smallholding that you want that is also eco-friendly too?

Reduce, Reuse, Recycle
A phrase made popular by the kid's TV show, Bob the Builder, this is something that applies to us all in the garden! Look at how you can make your smallholding self-sustainable from collecting rainwater, reducing energy use, recycling household items and more. Basically, it's about what can you reuse rather than throw away. For example, I use the cardboard insides of toilet rolls to start off my sweet peas and parsnips; cardboard egg boxes are used as seed cell trays and more. I've even seen old toilets and wellington boots used as planters and old baths can also make attractive planters!

Save Water
Water is a scarce resource, so you need to look after what you have in your smallholding! You may have a stream or river running through your property, but you have to be careful about using that water for your plants or animals as you do not know what is in it and do not want to use too much and impact the environment.

Collect rainwater where you can, which will help reduce your water bill and reliance on expensive, municipal water. Plant native or drought tolerant plants that need less watering and mulch your beds to retain moisture better. Water your plants early in the morning or late at night, which will significantly reduce water loss from evaporation. Water at the base of your plants so the water goes directly to the roots of the plants that need it.

Improve the Air Quality
Plants remove toxins and impurities from the air, improving its quality. Trees are particularly good at removing impurities from the air, but many other plants will do so too. Plant trees around your smallholding to act as windbreaks and fences. Plant an orchard of fruit trees and even, if you have the space, maintain a small area of woodland which will be ideal for wildlife and improving the air quality.

Reduce Electricity Usage
A lot of people have electricity in their smallholding running pumps or lights. Look at how you can reduce your reliance on electricity. Perhaps you can install solar powered lights and use solar panels to light your sheds. If you live in the right area, a small wind turbine can provide an easily source of clean energy. Use energy efficient lights and appliances wherever you can. Investigate geothermic energy for heating your home as that can be a big money saver and keep your running costs down.

Avoid Chemicals
Although there are organic chemicals you can use in your garden, many of these are still chemicals. Avoid as many chemicals as you can, but there are some situations where there isn't a lot of options and you do need to resort to the chemicals to destroy serious infestations of pests or bad cases of diseases.

Where you can, use alternatives. Neem oil is a very effective pesticide and can be mixed with garlic infused water or natural dish soap to increase its effectiveness. Use crushed egg shells, ground coffee beans and similar substances to protect your plants from slugs and snails.

Use companion planting to help the plants protect each other and further reduce your requirement for chemicals. Plant to attract predatory insects such as lady birds which will eat pests.

Compost
Some of your household waste and much of your garden waste can be composted. This will break down and then you can use it in your garden. Doing this prevents it going to landfill and creates a fantastic compost which is great for your plants ... plus it means you don't need to go out and buy compost! It's simple to do and has a large environmental impact.

Avoid composting weed seeds and perennial weeds such as dandelion, horse tail and docks because they often do not break down fully in a compost pile and will grow when you use the compost.

As a smallholder, you are going to use a lot of compost, so if you can make some of your own, then it will help save you money and time buying it in.

Synthetic Fertilisers
Many of these are manufactured using the 'Haber Bosch' process which converts methane, from natural gas, into hydrogen. The by-product of this is carbon dioxide that causes global warming. Making your own compost is much more environmentally friendly.

However, not everyone has the space or compostable material to create enough compost for their needs, but you can buy ecologically sound compost. Look for compost that has been produced by natural means. If your local city or council collects food waste, then they will be composting it. Often they will sell this to the public. This tends to be environmentally friendly because it is piled up, turned and allowed to compost naturally. The regular turning of the compost heats it up so that it breaks down rapidly and gets rid of most undesirable plant parts.

If you compost as much plant material as you can on your smallholding and the animal manure, then you can produce a good quantity of compost yourself. Although this may not be enough for your needs, it can certainly help.

Peat Based Compost

Across the world there are peat bogs, which lock large amounts of carbon dioxide into the ground. These peat bogs are being decimated as they are dug up and used for compost. This releases carbon dioxide into the atmosphere and prevents the peat bog from storing more of this harmful gas. In some countries, peat bogs are now being protected and allowed to re-establish themselves.

A significant amount of commercial compost contains peat harvested from these peat bogs. If you are going to buy compost, buy compost that is certified as peat free so that you are not contributing to this environmental problem. A coir compost is also very good as this is made from the waste product from processing coconuts. To make a compost hold moisture better, buy sphagnum moss and dig that into the soil as it works well.

Water Efficiency

Water efficiency is another big topic if you want to be environmentally friendly. With rising water bills, using water in your smallholding can quickly become expensive, as you could end up using a lot of it. You have to consider the environmental impact of processing water and transporting it to your home, particularly when it falls out of the sky (at least in some areas) for free!

Firstly, look at how and when you are watering your plants. Many people will use a hose for convenience, yet the water tends to go all over the place and you use more than you need because of a lack of direction. Sprinklers do an effective job of watering plants, but use an eye watering around of water! Watering cans are much more water efficient, though more work. With a watering can, you can direct the water to the base of your plant and ensure it gets the water it needs while not watering areas that do not need it. However, on a smallholding, watering cans are just not practical due to the sheer size of the area you are working on. They are great for the home garden, but not the best idea for the smallholder. A sprinkler can be used, but it uses a massive amount of water and the water is not directed to the plants.

When using a hose, make sure you use a spray gun with a trigger so you can target and control the water better. When not directly watering a plant, release the trigger to stop water going everywhere. The benefit of this is that only the plants you want get water and the weeds have to struggle on whatever water they can scavenge.

Water in the morning or late at night, which will reduce water lost through evaporation. If you can get it directly to the roots of the plant, then this reduces run-off and wasted water. If watering late at night, be very careful watering squash plants as water on the leaves can cause powdery mildew. It is important that members of the squash family are watered directly to the roots to reduce the risk of powdery mildew forming.

Pay attention to how much water each of your plants need and water them when they need it rather than just watering for the sake of it. Many plants do not need watering every day and are quite happy to be watered every few days. This alone will save a lot of water.

Using Water Butts
Every year, thousands of litres of water will fall on the average roof, and most of this goes down the drain and disappears. This eco-friendly source of water is one that is well worth capturing because you can use it to water your plants. It can help you save a bit of money, and every penny counts on a smallholding.

Install water butts on each of your drain downpipes on your buildings, making sure each one has a lid to stop insects, animals and leaves falling in to it. If you have the space, install multiple butts on each downpipe and use connector kits to link them together. You can store a surprising amount of water in these butts and it is actually better for your plants because it doesn't contain the chemicals found in your mains water supply.

Grey Water
Grey water is water that has been used in the home and can be re-used in the garden. This includes water from your shower, sink or laundry, but not from your toilet. Houses can be built with grey water recovery systems where this water is stored for use in the garden or for flushing the toilet, but these systems are not wide spread at present.

Water from boiling vegetables can be cooled and used to feed vegetable plants. This water is full of nutrients and really good for your plants. Water from baths, showers and washing up can be cooled and used to water non-edible plants.

You could even install a water butt near your kitchen door to pour this water into for when you want to use it. You might be surprised at just how much water you can reuse. However, due to the distance you would have to carry it, grey water on a smallholding is only really practical to use on plants near to the home.

Poorly Insulated Greenhouses/Polytunnels

If you are heating your greenhouse so you can grow exotic plants or grow in winter months, then you will have a larger than normal carbon footprint. Most greenhouses are single glazed and generally quite leaky so a lot of the heat escapes into the atmosphere. Generally, greenhouses are heated with paraffin heaters that release carbon dioxide.

Look at better insulating your greenhouse or using double glazing to keep the heat in. Alternatively, start your plants off indoors under full spectrum, LED grow lights that are very economical to run. You don't need to stop growing the plants you like, but look at ways to make your growing environment more environmentally sound.

If you are growing indoors, look at how you can better insulate the areas you are growing in and use power efficient lighting or heating. All of this can save you money and keep your running costs down.

Locally Sourced and Natural Products

Much of the carbon footprint from smallholding comes from buying products that are transported halfway around the planet. This can be anything from compost through to tools. Look carefully at what you buy and where it is coming from before you make the purchase. While this may not always be possible or affordable, particularly with our tendency to manufacture products in the Far East, any little thing you do makes a difference.

Look also at natural products and avoid plastics where you can. The more natural products you can use, the lower the associated carbon footprint, particularly when it comes to disposing of it. We can reduce our use of plastic, recycle anything possible and reuse waste material, more on all of this later on.

Natural Power Sources

If you use power in your garden for anything, can you use a renewable energy source rather than using mains electricity or gas/paraffin powered heating? Could you replace any of this with wind or solar power? If you use a petrol mower or strimmer, is there a more environmentally friendly option you can use instead such as sheep?

Think about how you are using power in your garden, particularly anything powered by fossil fuels. Could these be replaced with a more environmentally friendly source? Again, a single person making these changes doesn't have a large impact, but if a lot of people do, then potentially hundreds or even thousands of tons of carbon can be prevented from going into the atmosphere.

For a lot of smallholders, concern for the environment is high and they want to live in harmony with nature. Look at the activities you perform on your smallholding and how you can reduce the environmental impact of them. Even planting trees as hedges will help to reduce your environmental impact. If you can move to wind or solar energy, then this further increases your self-sufficiency and environmental friendliness. Starting a smallholding is a great way for you to decide to do more for the environment and live in closer harmony with nature.

Green Manures

Green manures are incredibly useful to grow, usually being sown towards the end of summer or autumn. The idea is that it locks nutrients into the soil, preventing them from being washed away in the winter rains. The following spring, the green manure is dug back into the soil where it breaks down and releases the nutrients back into the soil. A green manure can help prevent soil being washed away by rain and provide a habitat for beneficial insects. For the smallholder, this can be a great way to improve the soil while preventing weeds taking over.

If you have a bare patch of ground over winter or even space between crops or plants, then a green manure can be used to fill that space. Mustard, for example, grows very quickly and if planted by mid-September will be ready to be dug into the soil in October, or you can leave it to be killed off by frost and become a mulch.

There is summer grown green manures too, including fenugreek and buckwheat. These have very dense foliage that is an effective weed suppressant. Many gardeners will plant green manure rather than cover growing beds because they can add nutrients back to the soil.

Another type of green manure are legumes, which are members of the pea and bean family. The advantage of these, which I am sure you are aware of by now, is that they fix nitrogen into the soil which your next crop will benefit from.

I would not recommend planting a green manure in a bed where you don't have the weeds under control. If the area is infested with horse tail, bindweed or any other weed that spreads from its roots, then you can end up digging these weeds in and spreading them around. Remove all perennial weeds from the ground before planting green manure to ensure you get the most from it.

Using Green Manures

Green manures are usually sown in rows or scattered over the soil. When you are ready to use that area, cut down the foliage and leave it for a few days to wilt. Then dig both the roots and the foliage into the top 10-12 inches of the soil.

Once you have dug in the green manure, leave the area for a minimum of two weeks before planting. Using the area too early can cause problems for your plants as the decaying green manure can hamper growth.

Be aware that a thick carpet of green manure can provide a haven for slugs and snails, so you may need to take extra preventative measures against these pests if you are growing vegetable nearby.

Types of Green Manure

There are a lot of different types of green manure and which you use will depend on several factors, including:

- What time of year you are sowing the green manure
- How long you are leaving the green manure in place
- Whether you want to fix nitrogen into the soil or suppress weeds

Choose the best green manure for your needs. Green manure seeds can be bought online or you can find them in large garden stores. Some common green manures include:

Alfalfa (*Medicago sativa*)

This is a member of the legume family and can be dug into the soil after a couple of months. In larger areas, it can be left for a year or two before being dug in. Farmers often use alfalfa as a green manure for fallow fields. Alfalfa is best sown between April and July and is ideal for alkaline soils. Some alfalfa seeds are injected with nitrogen fixing bacteria and so can be used to fix nitrogen into the soil.

Normal alfalfa seeds will not fix nitrogen into the soil.

Alsike Clover (*Trifolium hybridum*)
Another legume, this can be dug in after two or three months or, in larger areas, left for up to two years. It grows well in wet or acidic soils and is typically sown from April through to August.

Bitter Blue Lupin (*Lupinus angustifolius*)
This is a perennial flower, also a member of the legume family. It grows very well in soils that are light, sandy, or acidic. This is best sown between March and June, usually being left for two or three months before it is dug in.

Buckwheat (*Fagopyrum esculentum*)
This is a half-hardy annual plant that grows in spring and summer, usually sown between April and August. It grows very well in nutrient poor soils and is dug in after two or three months.

Crimson Clover (*Trifolium incarnatum*)
This perennial legume grows well in a light soil. It is sown anytime from March through to August, typically being dug in after two or three months. However, you can leave this green manure in the ground up until it flowers.

Essex Red Clover (*Trifolium pratense*)
A great perennial green manure that is ideal for loamy soils. It is sown between March and August, being dug in after two or three months or left for up to two years if required.

Fenugreek (*Trigonella foenum-graecum*)
An annual legume which is planted in the spring or summer. In the UK, it doesn't fix nitrogen into the soil but does in warmer climates. It is typically dug in after two or three months.

Grazing Rye (*Seale cereale*)
This green manure is ideal to improve soil structure and will overwinter well in most areas. It is sown anytime between August and November, being dug in the next spring.

STRUCTURES AND EQUIPMENT

As a smallholder, you will need a variety of equipment and structures to effectively run your smallholding. Exactly what you need will depend on the size of your land, what you are growing and what livestock you have.

If you are dedicating a lot of space to growing vegetables, then you could benefit from a tractor with a ploughing attachment. If you are keeping cattle, then a quad bike could be handy. At the very least you will need tools to dig your vegetable garden, but if this is going to be big, you need mechanical tools to reduce the amount of time and effort it takes to dig. You want to be efficient in your working so that your time is used well.

New equipment can cost a lot of money, which may well be beyond your reach when you are starting out. However, there is a lively market for second hand equipment and you can usually find the items you want for a fraction of the full price, particularly if you attend auctions and know what you are looking for.

Some of the equipment that you could benefit from includes:

Tractor

A tractor can be very useful for getting around your smallholding, but also to make tasks such as mowing, cutting hedges, planting seeds, ploughing and more easy. It is a big investment and will cost a lot of money, but if you are planning on mainly growing vegetables and plants, it will be a big time saver.

Manually sowing 20 acres of land will take a lot of time, but with a seeder dragged by a tractor, it quickly becomes an easy task. Tractors can tow a variety of items from ploughs to mowers, to hedge cutters and more. It is certainly worth considering due to the amount of time it will save you.

A drag harrow is also useful for your pastures as it stops the grass getting choked with thatch so it grows well and is better suited for your livestock to graze on.

A tipping trailer is also very helpful as it makes moving logs, straw, food, manure and more much easier. Second hand, a trailer will cost somewhere from £150-200.

The tractor doesn't have to be full size, a compact tractor will be perfect for your smallholding, just make sure you have somewhere to store it out of the weather.

Rotovator
A petrol driven rotovator can be a big timesaver for your vegetable beds and help turn the soil over if you don't have a tractor with a plough. You want a heavy duty one as it will get a lot of use, but it will save you a lot of time digging and turning soil. Before using a rotovator, remove all perennial weeds such as dock and dandelion otherwise the rotovator just cuts the roots up and new plants will grow.

One of these can be an excellent way to get started in your vegetable garden as digging even half an acre by hand is back breaking. As they are much cheaper than a tractor, it could be an affordable way to start turning the soil until your business can support a tractor.

Quad Bike
A quad bike or all-terrain vehicle could be an excellent way to get around your smallholding, depending on the size of it. If you get one with a trailer, it makes it easy for you to move plants, compost and even some animals around your smallholding. While initially walking up and down your smallholding will be fun and enjoyable, when you are doing it dozens of times a day and carrying heavy loads, you will appreciate one of these. Some all-terrain vehicles can drag tools behind them, such as harrows or seed spreaders.

Sit on Mower

If you haven't got a tractor with a mowing attachment, then a sit on mower is the next best thing. You are likely to have a lot of pasture and unless you have animals eating it, you will want to keep the grass at a reasonable length. A sit on mower is ideal for this as a Flymo just isn't going to cut it and the wire is unlikely to stretch far enough!

For anything more than a garden lawn, one of these is absolutely vital and a huge timesaver. The cut grass can be left in the field or composted. A used sit on mower will cost anywhere from £600-800 for one that is suitable for use on your smallholding. A good quality sit on mower will be able to cut grass up to about three feet tall, drag a harrow and tow a trailer with a load of up to around 750kg. A decent sit on mower can do some of the jobs a compact tractor does, but at a fraction of the cost.

Diggers

Depending on the condition of your smallholding, a digger might be a good investment, particularly if you need to dig drainage ditches or remove large tree stumps. While they are not so good for digging vegetable gardens, they are very useful for clearing scrubland and move large amounts of soil. A mini digger should be sufficient, but if you do not need one full time, look at hiring one when needed.

Fencing

You will need fencing around your smallholding to keep your animals in and other animals out. Hopefully, this will already be in place, but you will need to inspect all of it and replace/repair it where necessary. This can be a significant cost, but it is important it is done right. A post hole digger is essential if you are putting in a large section of fence.

You also need to put in the right type of fencing. Simple wooden fences are great as boundary markers, but if you are keeping animals such as sheep or chickens, then better quality fences are required to prevent them from escaping. In some cases, an electric fence could be beneficial to keep your animals in.

If your area suffers from rabbits and you want to keep them out of your vegetable garden, then you need to dig a wire mesh fence down 2-3 feet under the ground to prevent these pests from burrowing into your gardens. Trees such as hawthorn or blackthorn (sloe) are excellent along the edges of your property, but they still need a good quality fence underneath them to stop animals getting in or out.

Wood Chipper

The chances are you will end up with a lot of waste wood from cutting back or down trees. While you can burn some of this, an alternative it to chip it and then use the wood chippings on your smallholding. Wood chips make for a good mulch around plants to keep water in and weeds down. They are also ideal for paths between beds in your vegetable garden. Alternatively, they can be donated/sold to a local allotment group or piled and left to rot down.

Brush Cutter

A strimmer is used just to cut grass and is great for your lawn, whereas as a smallholder you need a brush cutter. This takes different blades as well as cord and can be used to cut back brambles and even small saplings. Keeping your smallholding neat and paths free from weeds will be almost impossible without a good quality brush cutter.

Look for one that has a harness and two handlebars that look like bicycle handlebars as they will be much easier for you to use. A 50cc engine is best for a smallholding, but the minimum you should buy is 30cc. Brand new, a brush cutter will cost in the region of £250. Remember you will also need appropriate safety gear such as steel toecap boots, anti-vibration gloves, high impact face protect and ear defenders.

Animal Equipment

If you are keeping animals then you will need equipment for them from structures such as shelters, to a livestock trailer for transportation and many other things. Depending on the animals you are keeping, you will need feeders, water troughs/bowls, water systems and more.

Tools

Tools are essential not just for your vegetable garden and working on your smallholding, but for maintaining the structures of the smallholding itself.

For the vegetable garden you will need a spade, fork, hoe, rake and a set of hand tools too. A wheelbarrow is also very helpful, though make sure you get a good quality one, ideally with a puncture proof tyre. Your wheelbarrow will get a lot of use, so it is worth buying a good one.

You will also need a set of tools for DIY, working on your home and working on vehicles on your smallholding. You may already have most of these, but it is always handy to make sure you have the tools you need.

Electric Tools
Electric tools are going to be a big timesaver around the smallholding. Ideally you want battery or petrol powered tools because you don't want to be dragging a generator around your smallholding or running wires across buildings.

You do not need all of these from day one, but they are things to buy as and when you come across a job where you need them. Always go for the best quality you can afford because the tools will generally last longer. Make sure you look after them and clean them after use to keep them in good working order.

Greenhouse/Polytunnel
A greenhouse and or a polytunnel is essential on a smallholding as somewhere to start seeds off and to grow tender plants that would otherwise struggle to mature outside. At the very least you want one or the other, but if you can get both, or more than one, then that is going to help you as you will soon realise you need lots of space in these structures.

Your smallholding may already come with one of these. If not, or you need more, then you can often find them for sale second hand, though that usually means you have to dismantle them. A home sized greenhouse will be great for your vegetable garden to grow plants for your family, but if you are growing vegetables to sell, then you will need a much larger, industrial size greenhouse. Remember that wherever you decide to put these, make sure it is not under trees or anywhere that it can easily be damaged by flying debris.

Second hand greenhouses can be difficult to take down, and require a lot of patience and care. You will need gloves, WD-40, spanners, screwdrivers and pliers at the very least. Take lots of pictures before you take the greenhouse down and label all of the parts so it is easier for you to put it back together again. It will be easier if you have one or two people to help you with this task. For larger greenhouses, a ladder will be helpful so you can reach the roof easily. Be very careful transporting the glass and be prepared to replace some of the panes as they are likely to get broken.

Reassembling is a big job and you will need to have the base prepared before you start assembly. Again, you will need help to do this and you can expect it to take some time. When you reassemble it you will be very grateful that you labelled the parts and tool plenty of pictures.

Polytunnels are much more susceptible to wind damage than greenhouses, but greenhouses can also be damaged in high winds. They need a proper base and to be secured down properly to prevent wind damage. Take time to do this properly because if spring storms damage them while your seedlings are inside, it can ruin your potential to plant for the year, which can devastate your income opportunities.

You will need staging in both a greenhouse and polytunnel to put plants on. While you can plant direct in the soil, a lot of people put down flagstones and then plant in containers as it helps keep weeds down and prevents the soil getting exhausted.

Using containers provides a bit more flexibility and helps reduce your work as you are not caring for the soil within the structure as well as everything outside too.

Air circulation is important in both structures because otherwise your plants can overheat and die. As the weather warms up, open doors and windows to allow fresh air in and to help stop the temperatures rising too high so they damage your plants.

A greenhouse or polytunnel will be very important to you because they extend the growing season. It means you can start plants off from seed much earlier, and keep them safe from poor spring weather until the risk of frost has passed and they can be planted out. Come autumn when the weather is cooling, the same plants are still protected and in a warm environment so the fruit can fully ripen. In most parts of the UK, plants such as chillies, peppers, tomatoes, cucumbers and aubergines all benefit from being grown in a greenhouse as they have quite a long growing season.

Keeping your structures well maintained is important because it helps extend their life and keep them functioning well. Greenhouses in particularly need the glass cleaning every year so that it lets in as much light as possible.

Disinfect inside your structures at the end of each growing season to prevent the build-up of pests. Spider mites and other bugs can overwinter inside your greenhouse/polytunnel and become a major problem the following year.

A greenhouse is very important for a smallholder because it helps you grow vegetables which you are going to eat and perhaps sell. Well maintained, one will last for years, extending your growing season and helping you grow plants you would otherwise struggle to grow outside.

Sheds/Buildings

Your smallholding may come with some outbuildings. Which they are will depend on the smallholding, but the larger the property, the more buildings you will need. You need somewhere to store tools, equipment, harvests, vehicles and even shelter some animals from the elements.

Buildings where you are storing tools and equipment need to be secure in case of break in, plus you will need appropriate insurances to protect your equipment. Workshops and animal buildings need electricity and benefit from water being run to them, though this will depend on the cost and convenience.

All buildings require regular maintenance and looking after. Depending on the initial state of the buildings when you take on the smallholding, you may have to do a lot of this up front, so make sure you budget for it.

Out in the pastures, you may need temporary structures to shelter animals or to keep animal food out of the elements. A shed near your vegetable plot is convenient for storing tools so you are not having to walk too far every time you need a different tool.

If you want to put up new buildings, then make sure you are familiar with all the planning regulations before you start building. If you are not, you could end up having problems with the local authority, which ends up with more hassle for you and potentially a financial impact.

If you have outbuildings that you want to convert to holiday lets, contact your local authority before you start work. Many authorities require planning permissions for change of use of a building. When you buy a smallholding, your conveyancer should check the planning permission on all buildings already on the property.

Larger smallholdings are likely to have several buildings already in place, depending on the type of property and what it has been used for. The type of buildings already on a smallholding may influence what you choose to do on it. Although you may want to keep cattle, if you have to build a cattle shed, this is a major expense and one that you may not be able to afford initially. It may be that your idea of keeping cattle has to wait until you have the money to buy the equipment and put up the buildings.

When you visit a smallholding with a view to buying, look around all the structures to see the condition they are in, how much work they need doing and if they can be repurposed for the uses you have in mind for them. The structures add a lot of value to a smallholding and will be important as you start to run the smallholding.

Earning An Income From Your Smallholding

There are a lot of potential commercial activities you can undertake as a smallholder, many of which will depend on where your smallholding is located. If you are located in a tourist hotspot, then tourist related activities will be profitable. If you are located somewhere less tourist friendly, focusing on farmer's markets and other income streams makes much more sense.

Fruits and vegetables, meat, dairy, honey, eggs, firewood, plants and more are good sources of income. Letting extra rooms as a bed and breakfast business can be a good source of income in a tourist area. Alternatively, some outbuildings can be converted into holiday chalets or you could offer glamping holidays in yurts, tipis, treehouses or something similar. Glamping has become very popular and attracts a premium rate, so if you are in a desirable area of the country, this can be a very good source of income.

Before you buy a smallholding, you need to determine what the potential sources of income can be. This depends on your skills as well as what the local area will support. It may mean that you need to undertake some training, such as taking a beekeeping course or livestock handling course.

We have already discussed some potential sources of income earlier in this book where you learned about ideas on what you can grow on your smallholding and about keeping livestock. There are a lot of potential sources of income, but you need to focus on one or two at a time until they are fully developed and then move on to the next idea. Trying to take on too much at once will often result in nothing actually getting completed and your income streams fail to produce the income they should.

However, the maxim "If you build it, they will come" only applies to ghostly baseball fields and not to a smallholding. Customers are not going to come to you, but you will need to come to the customers, at least initially until you can build a reputation locally and people start to come to you, at which point a farm shop or other point of sale on your smallholding becomes a good idea.

One thing that is very important in your smallholding business is that you treat people fairly. In small communities, people talk and word quickly gets around. If you are overpriced, rip people off or provide poor quality goods and services, then this will soon become common knowledge and it can ruin your chances of generating income. It is much harder to overcome a poor reputation than it is to create a good reputation from the start. Your reputation is very important to you, so you need to ensure that you are firm, but fair and nice, though not so people take advantage of you. You are in business and need to make money to support your family, but by being fair and producing high quality produce, the local community will rally round and support you, particularly if you make an effort to become a part of that community.

Advertising

Whatever aspect of business you are in, you need to advertise to make customers aware of you and to spend money with you. Locally grown produce has seen demand increase significantly in recent years. Villages in particular shun large supermarkets and prefer to buy as much as they can locally, so selling produce, meat or locally made products can be a great source of income.

However, you need the customers to be able to find you. This means advertising and making people aware of your business. Many people find advertising hard, but it is something that you can learn and you can do it well at minimal cost to help boost your business.

You can make roadside signs advertising your business, have leaflets delivered to local houses or advertise in the local post office or shop.

You can also advertise online. Depending on what you are doing, and this is particularly important when it comes to holiday lets, you can set up a webpage or a Facebook page promoting your business. For holiday lets, this is vital as people want to see what it is they are going to be staying in. Make sure that the photographs you use online are the best quality possible. If you do not feel comfortable taking them yourself or you do not have a good enough camera, then hire a photographer or look for a local photography student who to do it for you.

Local farmer's markets are a great place to sell produce and hand-made goods. Use this as an opportunity to promote your business by handing out flyers or business cards to both customers and browsers. Ultimately, if you can get these people to come to you, then it makes your life easier and increase your profit margins.

High Value Items and Adding Value

A punnet of strawberries can only sell for so much, but you can increase the value of the strawberries by making them into something more valuable such as jam, ice cream or a pie. By processing what you produce on your smallholding into something more valuable, you can increase your profit margins and appeal to a different segment of the market.

Investigate the local market and see what the high value opportunities are in the area. Perhaps there are high-end restaurants nearby that are looking for fresh herbs, microgreens or vegetables to serve to their customers. Maybe you like keeping chickens and could add some quails to your flock because quail eggs sell for more money than chicken eggs.

Are the local people keen gardeners and would they appreciate a local source of plants for their gardens? You could start a plant nursery and sell bedding plants or perennials to the locals.

Could you grow some rare or unusual plants or vegetables? These command a premium price, but have a very specific market. Another potential idea is to become an expert on a single type of vegetable and focus on doing that extremely well. One example is a farm on the Isle of White which specialises in garlic, producing many different varieties each year which they sell online. Chillies are another great thing to grow, particularly the really hot or unusual varieties. These can be sold as is, dried, made into powder, turned into sauce or sold as living plants. People love chillies and will spend a lot of money buying unusual or super-hot plants.

Rare plants such as carnivorous plants or orchids are another potential way to make money. As these are difficult to get hold of, people will travel a long way to buy good quality plants and pay a premium for unusual or good quality plants. The key here is for you to advertise your business so that customers can find you.

Maybe you can craft items to sell such as carving wood, making Christmas decorations or similar things. These command a higher price, but they do require more work from you. However, this sort of items on a market stall can often attract people to you and encourage them to buy other things.

Knowing what the local market wants and what seasonal events occur locally helps you to produce products the market wants.

Curing meats, making chutneys, knitting with your wool and other ideas can turn your raw produce into something that is hand crafted and has a higher value. For example, you can sell your wool as wool, but also sell items that you have created from the wool. This then leads to you selling other items that go with wool such as knitting patterns, needles and similar paraphernalia, all of which can help attract people to your business and make you money.

Another advantage of this is that the products you make have a longer shelf life than the raw materials. Soft fruits have a very short shelf life, but if you make them into a jam, they can last for months. This has a big advantage for you as it reduces costly wastage and can give you something to sell out of season.

Unused Space

If you have outbuildings or garages that you are not using, what about renting them out so they become a source of income instead of a dumping ground?

Many small businesses and sole traders need space to work but do not want traditional office space because of the cost. All they need is a workshop or small office. Many local tradesmen or hobbyist would love a space like that.

If you think this is something you would like to pursue, the buildings could be converted into proper office or workshop space. Many small companies like office space in a quiet location, and it can be a steady source of income as no business likes to move regularly. If you can provide high speed broadband and good facilities, then the companies are going to be good earners for many years.

Another alternative, which involves more work, is to set up a cattery or kennels in your buildings. These can be excellent earners and a good business all year round. People love their pets and will pay good money for them to

An Introduction to Smallholdings

be well looked after in good accommodation while they go on holiday.

There is potential to turn unused bedrooms into bed and breakfast rooms or outbuildings into holiday chalets, which requires a higher initial investment. These can be a very good source of income, though be prepared to provide breakfast unless you are providing self-contained chalets.

Unused field space can be rented out as well. You can turn it into paddocks and rent it out to horse owners. This is another good, steady source of income, though you need to provide water to the paddocks and stables would add value and provide essential shelter.

Another use for land is to turn some of it into allotments and rent it out to the local community. While this is not going to be a big earner and the land is tied up long term, it is a good way to become part of the local community as allotment space is limited and in high demand.

Other activities

Can you offer activities on your smallholding that people will pay for? The best thing about a smallholding is that you can turn any interest or hobby of yours into a potential source of income. If you like archery, could you offer archery training or days?

If you keep animals and end up with a lot of compost, you can sell this as many home gardeners will pay good money for locally produced, good quality compost.

If you are offering accommodation on your smallholding, could you run courses or offer experience days where people help with the animals and experience what it is like to run a smallholding. You could offer a home-cooked meal made from ingredients you have grown to guests staying with you or for experience days.

Can you offer activities for major holidays like Easter, Christmas and Hallowe'en? There is a farm that specifically keeps and breeds reindeer, which they rent out to movie and TV companies, but at Christmas, they offer Santa experiences on site. Another smallholding has unusual animals like giraffes, zebra and more (which are an unusual site when driving through the countryside). These are also rented out to movie/TV companies. Offering activities around holidays allows you to sell your products but also sell ancillary products relating to the holiday.

Vegetable Boxes

Once you have your smallholding up and running and are producing fruit and vegetables all year round, you could set up your own vegetable box scheme. If you are producing meat, eggs or dairy products, these can also be included in the scheme.

Vegetable box schemes are very popular, though you will need to deliver them and set a delivery radius. These are very popular, particularly if you are in driving distance of a large city.

Typically, you offer different sizes of vegetable box at different price points with extras such as meat, eggs or dairy costing more. These are delivered once a week and will contain whatever you have ripe at that time. Items such as potatoes will store for months, so you can keep these in storage and offer them all year around. Other produce is usually offered when it is in season. With a greenhouse or polytunnel, you can grow enough for a vegetable box all year round.

This is something you can collaborate on with other smallholders to provide a good selection of produce throughout the year.

Have the Right Protection

Nobody likes to talk about insurance, but it is something that is extremely important for your protection.

Running a smallholding has risks, you have to be realistic about it. If there is a crop failure, then you may struggle to feed yourself or fulfil orders or have anything to sell at the market. If your animals get ill, then that can impact your meat, egg or dairy production, which could affect your income. What if your tractor breaks down or your electricity goes out and the freezers you store your food in break?

Insurance is a complex business, with the smallholder wanting as little insurance as possible and the insurance companies wanting to insure you for absolutely everything regardless of the cost.

Smallholder insurance is specialist and you will need to contact a specialist company to ensure you get the right insurance. While there are several companies you could use, the NFU Mutual are a good company to talk to.

The insurance provides you and your family with a safety net and can help protect against income loss, critical illness and more. If you are running the smallholding and bringing in the money, you need to think about what happens to your family if you are unable to work. It is not something any of us like to think about, but you do need to think about it and protect yourself and your family. As the Covid-19 crisis of 2020 proved, nothing is certain and calamity can strike at any time.

ENDNOTE

A smallholding is a big undertaking and a major life change, so it is something that you have to really think about and plan before making the leap. It is something that more and more people are considering as they evaluate their lives and decide they want to escape the rat race and live more in harmony with nature.

The first step is to look at your budget and finances so you know how much you can afford to spend, what your running costs will be and how you will cover those costs.

Next you need to decide what you must have on your smallholding and what are just nice to have features. Once you know this, then you can start looking at properties either all over the country or in the area(s) you want to live in. Knowing what you want from a smallholding will help you decide whether or not one is right for you. If you do not want to deal with the public and run a B&B or holiday lets, then there isn't much point buying a property with holiday cottages on.

Determine how much space you want and buy as much land as you can afford, because sooner or later you are bound to want more and then moving becomes a big deal, which you probably won't want to do. The extra land can be left fallow, planted as an orchard or even rented out to locals until you are ready to use it.

An Introduction to Smallholdings

There is a lot you can grow on your smallholding, either for your family as food or as a source of income. The key is to not try and take on too much at once. Take on just one or two major projects each year so that you do not get overwhelmed and can focus on making each project successful.

Remember that many potential income sources can take some time before they are actually earning any money, so you need to ensure you can survive in the meantime. Growing salads and microgreens are very quick sources of income, because they are ready to harvest quickly. Some smallholders use these rapidly maturing crops as sources of income while they work on longer term projects like growing vegetables, creating a Christmas tree farm and so on. It is important that you keep a close eye on your numbers and know exactly what you have coming in and going out. There is a lot you can do over time to reduce your outgoings as you become more self-sufficient.

Livestock is commonly kept on smallholdings, though what you will keep depends on your lifestyle, eating habits and your location. Larger animals such as cows take up a lot more space than chickens and require a lot more physical work and paperwork. As livestock is a big commitment, you need to think very carefully about it before you start. Fully investigate everything about keeping livestock from the paperwork to what equipment you need and how to care for them. Remember that you are going to need a lot of sturdy fencing for most livestock!

A big part of owning a smallholding is becoming more environmentally friendly. There is a lot you can do as a smallholder to become more eco-friendly, from reducing your plastic usage to using less chemicals or installing solar panels. What you do will depend on your budget, location and what you want to do. Even planting trees around the edge of your property will make a big difference and help sequester carbon.

A smallholding requires a lot of work and thought on your part. You need to be prepared for the work and the fact you may struggle to get away, particularly if you have livestock. It is a complete lifestyle change and is nothing like the TV series, "The Good Life". You will be out in the rain and snow tending your livestock and working on your plants or trees. However, it is incredibly rewarding and a big change from the rat race in a city.

Do as much research as you can before you take on a smallholding and even try to get some practise by taking some smallholding courses or something similar. Join online communities and start to understand the work and commitment involved. While it is a lot of work, it is very rewarding and very enjoyable. The lifestyle change suits many people and the freedom of being in charge of your own destiny is a wonderful feeling.

Once you take on a smallholding, the hard work begins, but so does the enjoyment. Many people say that getting up at 5am to catch a packed train to commute to an office to sit at a desk all day is soul destroying, but getting up at 5am to tend your flock of sheep and work in your vegetable garden is a joyous experience!

Enjoy researching smallholding and good luck in your move to becoming self-sufficient!

About Jason

Jason has been a keen gardener for over twenty years, having taken on numerous weed infested patches and turned them into productive vegetable gardens.

One of his first gardening experiences was digging over a 400 square foot garden in its entirety and turning it into a vegetable garden, much to the delight of his neighbors who all got free vegetables! It was through this experience that he discovered his love of gardening and started to learn more and more about the subject.

His first encounter with a greenhouse resulted in a tomato infested greenhouse but he soon learnt how to make the most of a greenhouse and now grows a wide variety of plants from grapes to squashes to tomatoes and more.

He is passionate about helping people learn to grow their own fresh produce and enjoy the many benefits that come with it, from the exercise of gardening to the nutrition of freshly picked produce. He often says that when you've tasted a freshly picked tomato you'll never want to buy another one from a store again!

Jason is also very active in the personal development community, having written books on self-help, including subjects such as motivation and confidence. He has also recorded over 80 hypnosis programs, being a fully qualified clinical hypnotist which he sells from his website www.MusicForChange.com.

He hopes that this book has been a pleasure for you to read and that you have learned a lot about the subject and welcomes your feedback either directly or through an Amazon review. This feedback is used to improve his books and provide better quality information for his readers.

Jason also loves to grow giant and unusual vegetables and is still planning on breaking the 400lb barrier with a giant pumpkin. He hopes that with his new allotment plot he'll be able to grow even more exciting vegetables to share with his readers.

Other Books By Jason

A Gardener's Guide to Weeds - How To Use Common Garden Weeds For Food, Health, Beauty And More
Ever wondered about the weeds that take over your garden? You may be surprised to know that these weeds are the ancestors of many of the crops we regularly eat and used to be the staple diet for humans. This book teaches you all about weeds including how to use them in your garden and kitchen and their traditional medicinal uses as well as the folklore and myths associated with them. A fascinating insight into the gardener's foe!

Berry Gardening – The Complete Guide to Berry Gardening from Gooseberries to Boysenberries and More
Who doesn't love fresh berries? Find out how you can grow many of the popular berries at home such as marionberries and blackberries and some of the more unusual like honeyberries and goji berries. A step by step guide to growing your own berries including pruning, propagating and more. Discover how you can grow a wide variety of berries at home in your garden or on your balcony.

Canning and Preserving at Home – A Complete Guide to Canning, Preserving and Storing Your Produce
A complete guide to storing your home-grown fruits and vegetables. Learn everything from how to freeze your produce to canning, making jams, jellies, and chutneys to dehydrating and more. Everything you need to know about storing your fresh produce, including some unusual methods of storage, some of which will encourage children to eat fresh fruit!

Companion Planting Secrets – Organic Gardening to Deter Pests and Increase Yield

Learn the secrets of natural and organic pest control with companion planting. This is a great way to increase your yield, produce better quality plants and work in harmony with nature. By attracting beneficial insects to your garden, you can naturally keep down harmful pests and reduce the damage they cause. You probably grow many of these companion plants already, but by repositioning them, you can reap the many benefits of this natural method of gardening.

Container Gardening - Growing Vegetables, Herbs & Flowers in Containers

A step by step guide showing you how to create your very own container garden. Whether you have no garden, little space or you want to grow specific plants, this book guides you through everything you need to know about planting a container garden from the different types of pots, to which plants thrive in containers to handy tips helping you avoid the common mistakes people make with containers.

Cooking with Zucchini - Delicious Recipes, Preserves and More With Courgettes: How To Deal With A Glut Of Zucchini And Love It!

Getting too many zucchinis from your plants? This book teaches you how to grow your own courgettes at home as well as showing you the many different varieties you could grow. Packed full of delicious recipes, you will learn everything from the famous zucchini chocolate cake to delicious main courses, snacks, and Paleo diet friendly raw recipes. The must have guide for anyone dealing with a glut of zucchini.

Environmentally Friendly Gardening – Your Guide to a Sustainable, Eco-Friendly Garden

With a looming environmental crisis, we are all looking to do our bit to save the environment. This book talks you through how to garden in harmony with nature and reduce your environmental impact. Learn how to eliminate the need for chemicals with clever techniques and eco-friendly alternatives. Discover today how you can become a more environmentally friendly gardener and still have a beautiful garden.

Greenhouse Gardening - A Beginners Guide to Growing Fruit and Vegetables All Year Round

A complete, step by step guide to owning your own greenhouse. Learn everything you need to know from sourcing greenhouses to building foundations to ensuring it survives high winds. This handy guide will teach you everything you need to know to grow a wide range of plants in your greenhouse, including tomatoes, chilies, squashes, zucchini and much more. Find out how you can benefit from a greenhouse today, they are more fun and less work than you might think!

Growing Brassicas – Growing Cruciferous Vegetables from Broccoli to Mooli to Wasabi and More

Brassicas are renowned for their health benefits and are packed full of vitamins. They are easy to grow at home but beset by problems. Find out how you can grow these amazing vegetables at home, including the incredibly beneficial plants broccoli and maca. Includes step by step growing guides plus delicious recipes for every recipe!

Growing Chilies – A Beginners Guide to Growing, Using & Surviving Chilies

Ever wanted to grow super-hot chilies? Or maybe you just want to grow your own chilies to add some flavor to your food? This book is your complete, step-by-step guide to growing chilies at home. With topics from selecting varieties to how to germinate seeds, you will learn everything you need to know to grow chilies successfully, even the notoriously difficult to grow varieties such as Carolina Reaper. With recipes for sauces, meals and making your own chili powder, you'll find everything you need to know to grow your own chili plants

Growing Fruit: The Complete Guide to Growing Fruit at Home

This is a complete guide to growing fruit from apricots to walnuts and everything in between. You will learn how to choose fruit plants, how to grow and care for them, how to store and preserve the fruit and much more. With recipes, advice, and tips this is the perfect book for anyone who wants to learn more about growing fruit at home, whether beginner or experienced gardener.

Growing Garlic – A Complete Guide to Growing, Harvesting & Using Garlic

Everything you need to know to grow this popular plant. Whether you are growing normal garlic or elephant garlic for cooking or health, you will find this book contains all the information you need. Traditionally a difficult crop to grow with a long growing season, you'll learn the exact conditions garlic needs, how to avoid the common problems people encounter and how to store your garlic for use all year round. A complete, step-by-step guide showing you precisely how to grow garlic at home.

Growing Herbs – A Beginners Guide to Growing, Using, Harvesting and Storing Herbs

A comprehensive guide to growing herbs at home, detailing 49 different herbs. Learn everything you need to know to grow these herbs from their preferred soil conditions to how to harvest and propagate them and more. Including recipes for health and beauty plus delicious dishes to make in your kitchen. This step-by-step guide is designed to teach you all about growing herbs at home, from a few herbs in containers to a fully-fledged herb garden. An indispensable guide to growing and using herbs.

Growing Giant Pumpkins – How to Grow Massive Pumpkins at Home

A complete step by step guide detailing everything you need to know to produce pumpkins weighing hundreds of pounds, if not edging into the thousands! Anyone can grow giant pumpkins at home, and this book gives you the insider secrets of the giant pumpkin growers showing you how to avoid the mistakes people commonly make when trying to grow a giant pumpkin. This is a complete guide detailing everything from preparing the soil to getting the right seeds to germinating the seeds and caring for your pumpkins.

Growing Lavender: Growing, Using, Cooking and Healing with Lavender

A complete guide to growing and using this beautiful plant. Find out about the hundreds of different varieties of lavender and how you can grow this bee friendly plant at home. With hundreds of uses in crafts, cooking and healing, this plant has a long history of association with humans. Discover today how you can grow lavender at home and enjoy this amazing herb.

Growing Tomatoes: Your Guide to Growing Delicious Tomatoes at Home

This is the definitive guide to growing delicious and fresh tomatoes at home. Teaching you everything from selecting seeds to planting and caring for your tomatoes as well as diagnosing problems this is the ideal book for anyone who wants to grow tomatoes at home. A comprehensive must have guide.

How to Compost – Turn Your Waste into Brown Gold

This is a complete step by step guide to making your own compost at home. Vital to any gardener, this book will explain everything from setting up your compost heap to how to ensure you get fresh compost in just a few weeks. A must have handbook for any gardener who wants their plants to benefit from home-made compost.

Hydroponics: A Beginners Guide to Growing Food without Soil
Hydroponics is growing plants without soil, which is a fantastic idea for indoor gardens. It is surprisingly easy to set up, once you know what you are doing and is significantly more productive and quicker than growing in soil. This book will tell you everything you need to know to get started growing flowers, vegetables, and fruit hydroponically at home.

Indoor Gardening for Beginners: The Complete Guide to Growing Herbs, Flowers, Vegetables and Fruits in Your House
Discover how you can grow a wide variety of plants in your home. Whether you want to grow herbs for cooking, vegetables or a decorative plant display, this book tells you everything you need to know. Learn which plants to keep in your home to purify the air and remove harmful chemicals and how to successfully grow plants from cacti to flowers to carnivorous plants.

Keeping Chickens for Beginners – Keeping Backyard Chickens from Coops to Feeding to Care and More
Chickens are becoming very popular to keep at home, but it isn't something you should leap into without the right information. This book guides you through everything you need to know to keep chickens from decided what breed to what coop to how to feed them, look after them and keep your chickens healthy and producing eggs. This is your complete guide to owning chickens, with absolutely everything you need to know to get started and successfully keep chickens at home.

Raised Bed Gardening – A Guide to Growing Vegetables In Raised Beds
Learn why raised beds are such an efficient and effortless way to garden as you discover the benefits of no-dig gardening, denser planting and less bending, ideal for anyone who hates weeding or suffers from back pain. You will learn everything you need to know to build your own raised beds, plant them and ensure they are highly productive.

Save Our Bees – Your Guide to Creating a Bee Friendly Environment
Discover the plight of our bees and why they desperately need all of our help. Find out all about the different bees, how they are harmless, yet a vital part of our food chain. This book teaches you all about bees and how you can create a bee friendly environment in your neighborhood. You will learn the plants bees love, where they need to live and what plants are dangerous for bees, plus lots, lots more.

Vertical Gardening: Maximum Productivity, Minimum Space
This is an exciting form of gardening allows you to grow large amounts of fruit and vegetables in small areas, maximizing your use of space. Whether you have a large garden, an allotment or just a small balcony, you will be able to grow more delicious fresh produce. Find out how I grew over 70 strawberry plants in just three feet of ground space and more in this detailed guide.

Worm Farming: Creating Compost at Home with Vermiculture
Learn about this amazing way of producing high-quality compost at home by recycling your kitchen waste. Worms break it down and produce a sought after, highly nutritious compost that your plants will thrive in. No matter how big your garden you will be able to create your own worm farm and compost using the techniques in this step-by-step guide. Learn how to start worm farming and producing your own high-quality compost at home.

Want More Inspiring Gardening Ideas?

This book is part of the Inspiring Gardening Ideas series. Bringing you the best books anywhere on how to get the most from your garden or allotment. Please remember to leave a review on Amazon once you have finished this book as it helps me continually improve my books.

You can find out about more wonderful books just like this one at: www.GardeningWithJason.com.

Follow me at www.YouTube.com/OwningAnAllotment for my video diary and tips. Join me on Facebook for regular updates and discussions at www.Facebook.com/OwningAnAllotment.

Find me on Instagram and Twitter as @allotmentowner where I post regular updates, offers and gardening news. Follow me today and let's catch up in person!

Free Book!

Visit http://gardeningwithjason.com/your-free-book/ now for your free copy of my book "Environmentally Friendly Gardening" sent to your inbox. Discover today how you can become a more eco-friendly gardener and help us all make the world a better place.

This book is full of tips and advice, helping you to reduce your need for chemicals and work in harmony with nature to improve the environment. With the looming crisis, there is something we can all do in our gardens, no matter how big or small they are and they can still look fantastic!

Thank you for reading!

Printed in Great Britain
by Amazon